MW01061224

your

D A I L Y

mental

VITAMIN

by

Garry Kinder

your *DAILY* *mental* VITAMIN

by
Garry Kinder

EMBASSY BOOKS
www.embassybooks.in

Your Daily Mental Vitamin

Copyright 2010 © by Kinder Brothers International

First Published in India: 2010

Published by:
EMBASSY BOOK DISTRIBUTORS
120, Great Western Building
Maharashtra Chamber of Commerce Lane
Fort, Mumbai-400 023 (India)
Tel: (+91-22) 22819546 / 32967415
Email: info@embassybooks.in
Website: www.embassybooks.in

Distributed in the U.S.A. by:
KINDER BROTHERS INTERNATIONAL
17110 Dallas Parkway, #220
Dallas, TX 75248 (USA)
Tel: 972-380-0747 or 800-372-7110
Email: kinders@kbigroup.com
Website: www.KBIgroup.com

All rights reserved. No part of this book may be used or reproduced in any manner whatsoever without written permission from the publishers, except in the case of brief quotations embodied In articles and reviews.

All scripture quotations are from the *Holy Bible, The King James* Version.

ISBN 13: 978-93-80227-37-5

Book and Cover Design: Namrata Chattaraj.

Printed and Bound in India by:
M/s. Decora Book Prints Pvt. Ltd., Mumbai

Foreword

Over the past few decades, almost everyone has become aware that vitamins are vital to a healthy physical body. What's less widely understood is the importance of supplementing our mental and spiritual bodies.

Now Garry Kinder, a successful businessman and public speaker, offers a year's worth of mental vitamins—easily digestible bits of wisdom to carry you through each day. The inspirations in this little book can help fortify your immune system against life's number one joy killer: negative thinking. Read a page daily and enjoy optimum mental health!

KEN BLANCHARD

Co-author of The One Minute Manager®

D A I L Y   m e n t

Acknowledgments

I want to thank my brother, Jack, who taught me many of these philosophies early in my career. Jack was disciplined in feeding his mind positive thoughts. He carried 3 x 5 cards with him to be sure and capture great words of wisdom he felt were worthy of memorizing.

I want to thank the countless individuals who have encouraged us with positive mental vitamins through the years.

I want to thank my wife, Janet, for her patience and support. She's always looking for uplifting, positive messages.

Thanks to Lu Ann Butler for her tireless effort in reading and editing this manuscript. She is a faithful employee of Kinder Brothers and a friend.

Thanks to Ken Blanchard for providing the Foreword for the book. His positive encouragement was a tremendous help in getting the book written. I appreciate his contributions!

VITAMIN

Endorsements

Everybody knows that a daily vitamin is good for the human body. The mental vitamin is what Garry Kinder is all about. The daily mental vitamin helps start every day with a positive attitude. After a 50-year relationship with him, I can say Garry Kinder practices what he preaches. (*KEN MILLER*)

All of us, regardless of our station in life, need a mental lift. This book will supply you with the resource to help you be at your best every day. Use the Mental Vitamins on a daily basis. (*ROGER STAUBACH*)

When I played in the NFL (1957-1968), Garry was my great friend! Before every game and even through the week we talked in person or on the phone and he always had some words of wisdom, "mental vitamins", to feed my motivational needs. I couldn't play my best without those vitamins. This book is a must for high achievers. You'll get hooked on these daily vitamins and grow stronger as a result of reading and, of course, applying these great power-packed motivators to your life! (*BILL GLASS*)

Garry Kinder's Mental Vitamin book is terrific. Our behavior is determined by our beliefs, and this book, read daily, will heighten your belief in your ability to get it done that day! Garry has compiled the finest such vehicle for achieving high performance through daily inspiration that I have seen. Get it and read it every day! (DON HUTSON) SPEAKER, AND CO-AUTHOR OF THE #1 NEW YORK TIMES BEST-SELLER, THE ONE MINUTE ENTREPRENEUR, AND CEO OF U. S. LEARNING, MEMPHIS, TN

Insight and encouragement abound in these pages. What Garry offers comes to you with triple-strength power: The power of truth, the power of proven performance, and the power of a life that validates the words. Read it, apply it and share it as fast as you can! (RICK LOY)

Garry Kinder is the single greatest encourager I have ever known. The Bible says, "As a man thinks in his heart so is he." These daily vitamins from Garry's pen will be a constant stimulus to reach beyond your grasp every day of the year and to...be encouraged! (O.S. HAWKINS)

Introduction

I've enjoyed putting these mental vitamins together; I trust you will enjoy taking them on a daily basis. Most everybody today takes some form of vitamin for their physical well being. All of us need mental vitamins, as well. This book was created to give you one daily mental vitamin to take along with your physical vitamins.

GARRY KINDER
Your Daily Mental Vitamin

1st
QUARTER

We start the 1st Quarter with
"Seven Laws for Leaders who Lead".
These daily mental vitamins are given to you
by my brother, Jack, and me.
These laws were written by us several years ago.

No matter what your station in life, you are a leader!

Law #1

REPUTATION CULTIVATION

[Jack and Garry Kinder - LAWS OF LEADERS WHO LEAD]

- Find the way to make good on all commitments.
  Form this belief: **A commitment made is a debt unpaid.**

- Goals are set to be met. Therefore, make good on all your
  goals throughout the year.

Law #2

WINNING

[Jack and Garry Kinder - LAWS OF LEADERS WHO LEAD]

Surround yourself with winners. Whether it's in business or your personal life, be determined to engage with people who know where they are going.

Law #3

RELATIONSHIP BUILDING

[Jack and Garry Kinder - LAWS OF LEADERS WHO LEAD]

Encourage all of your friends and associates. Be known as an encourager. Help others believe the best about themselves; you will help them move toward a successful future.

Law #4

EFFECTIVENESS

[Jack and Garry Kinder - LAWS OF LEADERS WHO LEAD]

Never confuse activity with accomplishment.

A person walking around in circles is working just as hard as the person going down the street – one is getting dizzy; the other is going somewhere.

Law #5

MAXIMIZATION

[Jack and Garry Kinder - LAWS OF LEADERS WHO LEAD]

Consistently monitor and measure those few things that matter
– what matters will improve.

In everything you do, know the score, keep the score and the
score will improve.

Law #6

PERSONAL GROWTH

[Jack and Garry Kinder - LAWS OF LEADERS WHO LEAD]

Read and inwardly digest one book each month. Feed the mind as you feed the body. Leaders are readers and readers are leaders.

Law #7

LONGEVITY

[Jack and Garry Kinder - LAWS OF LEADERS WHO LEAD]

Enjoy the rewards that can be yours by focusing on and excelling in the things you can control.

Work on those things you can control. Strive to have peace with those things you can't control.

KNOWING WHERE YOU'RE GOING IS THE FIRST STEP TO GETTING THERE.

[Ken Blanchard]

Have you identified your mission in life – your reason for being? Establishing a personal mission statement is an important exercise that has helped me define who I am, identify my priorities, and keep my perspective on target. It involves identifying your passions.

I've noticed that I'm happiest and at my best when I'm teaching or writing. I also want to make a difference in other people's lives. Therefore my mission statement reads: To be a loving teacher and example of simple truths that help myself and others to awaken the presence of God in our lives. I say "awaken the presence of God" because I am constantly encouraging myself and others to get our egos out of the way so God can do His work. Remember "EGO" really stands for "Edging God Out."

Look inside yourself and let God help you find the driving force in your life. Doing so is the first step to a happier and more satisfied you.

[Excerpt from The Heart of a Leader, Ken Blanchard]

THE TRAGEDY IN LIFE DOESN'T LIE IN NOT REACHING YOUR GOAL; THE TRAGEDY LIES IN HAVING NO GOAL TO REACH.

[Benjamin Mays]

Goals are the starting point of all achievement. People without goals are like a ship without a rudder.

Set goals that are attainable and go after them every day.

WELL BEGUN IS HALF DONE.

[Greek Proverb]

Momentum is everything. Big First Quarter! Big Year!

Big Monday! Big Week! The first business day of the week should be the best business day of the week.

Fast starters are fast finishers. In everything you do, get off the mark fast.

THE PERSON WHO MAKES A SUCCESS
OF LIVING IS THE ONE WHO SEES
HIS GOAL STEADILY AND AIMS FOR IT
UNSWERVINGLY. THAT IS DEDICATION.

[Cecille B. DeMille]

Be steadfast, be unswerving in reaching your goal. Keep it in
front of you at all times.

Following the 2008 Olympics, where swimmer Michael Phelps
won a record-breaking eight Gold Medals, I found out that he
had all of his goals written out and with him at all times.

TODAY I WILL MULTIPLY MY VALUE A HUNDREDFOLD.

[Og Mandino - Scroll #VIII - The Greatest Salesman in the World]

Setting goals will help you multiply your value exponentially.

Og Mandino said, "Never will I be of concern that my goals are too high, for is it not better to aim my spear at the moon and strike only an eagle than to aim my spear at the eagle and strike only a rock? Never be content with your performance."

THE QUALITY OF A PERSON'S LIFE
IS IN DIRECT PROPORTION TO THEIR
COMMITMENT TO EXCELLENCE,
REGARDLESS OF THEIR CHOSEN FIELD OF
ENDEAVOR.

[Vince Lombardi]

Strategies for reaching and maintaining high standards of
excellence:

- Develop professional competency.
- Join a study group.
- Think bigger.
- Keep educationally active.
- Write articles.

We never drift into excellence. We must cultivate standards of
excellence – they do not spontaneously emerge.

EXPECT THE BEST!

[Ken Blanchard]

You've heard it said, "What you see is what you get."

Consider this alternative: "What you expect is what you get."
Expect great things of yourself. Expect high achievement.
Expect the best!

Bumblebees don't know it is aerodynamically impossible for
them to fly. They simply expect it of themselves! What do
you expect of yourself? Are you like the bumblebees who
don't know they can't? Or do you limit yourself by staying
within restrictive boundaries?

YOUR CALENDAR AND YOUR CHECKBOOK REFLECT YOUR PRIORITIES.

[Howard Wight]

Focus on the task at hand. Eliminate distractions. Put the blinders on and go down "Main Street". Focus on what you need to accomplish today.

IF THE FUTURE WERE GUARANTEED, WHAT WOULD YOU DO RIGHT NOW TO MAKE IT HAPPEN? DO THAT!

[Tom Stat - Business developer and innovation expert]

Put away the doubt and take the first step toward the future you desire. Act as if you cannot fail.

Every day of your life, see yourself succeeding in the things you are doing. Believe you can, and you will.

Success comes in "can's", not "can not's".

17

FOR UNTO WHOMSOEVER MUCH IS GIVEN,
OF HIM SHALL BE MUCH REQUIRED: AND
TO WHOM MEN HAVE COMMITTED MUCH,
OF HIM THEY WILL ASK THE MORE.

[Jesus - Luke 12:48 - KJV]

Goals are the starting point of all achievement. People without
goals are like a ship without a rudder.

Set goals that are attainable and go after them every day.

PUT OFF PROCRASTINATING!

Do you have the tendency to procrastinate? If you do, you are a person who has mastered the art of keeping up with yesterday.

Memorize this: Success is the product of today's responsibilities fulfilled, today's opportunities seized, and today's jobs handled.

Promise yourself your work will be done today, the unpleasant tasks will be cleared up today.

Today you owe it to yourself, your family, and your organization to break loose from the bonds of procrastination and discover the immediate rewards of accomplishing today – achieving today.

IF YOU WANT TO MAKE AN EASY JOB SEEM MIGHTY HARD, JUST KEEP PUTTING OFF DOING IT.

[Olin Miller]

The longer you wait, the harder it gets. The hardest part is getting started.

W. Clement Stone taught us: Do it now! Don't put it off, do it now.

Solomon taught us, "With all thy getting, get understanding." Jesus said, "With all thy getting, get going." To many a sinner he said, "Go and sin no more." To his disciples he said, "Go into the world and give them the message –the good news."

HONEST, INTELLIGENT EFFORT IS ALWAYS REWARDED.

Between the person you are and the person you'd like to be lies your constant struggle.

Have you observed that successful people are doers? They motivate themselves to do what it takes to get the job done. They are self-starters and self-promoters.

An honest day's work is your moral obligation. Here are three keys for putting in an honest day's work:

1. Do the right activities!
2. Do them right!
3. Do them often!

THE MORE EXTENSIVE A MAN'S KNOWLEDGE OF WHAT HAS BEEN DONE, THE GREATER WILL BE HIS POWER OF KNOWING WHAT TO DO.

[Benjamin Disraeli]

Success always hangs out around knowledge.

Constantly be studying so you can perform better in your job. Knowledge is not necessarily power, but knowledge in action is power.

THERE IS NO SUBSTITUTE FOR PAYING ATTENTION.

Develop the habit of paying attention. Decide to be a shrewd observer.

All things being equal, it is the keen observer who moves ahead. No matter where you go, study the situation. Make important deductions from what you see and hear. Let nothing escape you.

Most people don't see things; they merely look at them. They listen, but do not hear.

Paying attention is a powerful mental process. It will keep your mind on the material that the eyes and ears bring it.

FAIL FORWARD.

Put failure to work for you. Difficulties bring out your best qualities and make greatness possible.

Subscribe to this philosophy: "Fail Forward; It's Always Too Early to Give Up."

It's not what happens to you, but what you do after it happens that makes the big difference. People who grow and rise to the top are those who use difficulty to their advantage, rather than simply trying to avoid it.

NO PERSON IS WHAT HE THINKS HE IS, BUT WHAT HE THINKS – HE IS.

[Robert Anthony]

Self-talk shapes your life. What you are is the result of the many accumulated statements you have made and continue to make with your self-talk.

What have you told yourself today? What conversation has gone on in your head or been spoken aloud?

Take charge of your thoughts. They are yours to control. Monitor what you are telling yourself about your potential.

MAKE EVERY OCCASION A GREAT OCCASION.

You never know when someone is taking your measure for a higher position.

Every occasion — even an unwanted, time-consuming interruption — can be transformed into a great occasion.

How? Simply by viewing the event through the lens of an expectant, determined, creative attitude.

No occasion is a "little" occasion. No moment is insignificant. No person is unimportant. This appointment, this doctor's visit, this presentation, this situation can become a great occasion, if you choose to make it so!

DO IT . . . AND THEN SOME.

We're convinced these three little words – **and then some** – make the difference between average people and top performers, no matter what their occupation.

You may be just a short distance from success in your career. Just a little improvement in your daily planning, a little adjustment in your presentation, a little additional knowledge, a little more positive action, or persistence – and unusual success can become yours.

High achievers do what is expected – **and then some.**

HE THAT IS FAITHFUL IN THAT WHICH IS
LEAST IS FAITHFUL ALSO IN MUCH: AND
HE THAT IS UNJUST IN THE LEAST IS
UNJUST ALSO IN MUCH.

[Jesus - Luke 16:10 - KJV]

No matter how small a task, always do what you are supposed
to do – and then some.

He that is faithful in little things will be faithful in big things.

IT IS BETTER TO DIE FOR SOMETHING THAN TO LIVE FOR NOTHING.

We live our lives to the fullest. It is important to get caught up in a cause or a purpose greater than ourselves.

Once we know our purpose, we need to continue to develop a passion for our purpose.

LOSERS TALK ABOUT WHAT THEY ARE
GOING THROUGH. WINNERS TALK ABOUT
WHAT THEY ARE GOING TO. NEVER
CONFUSE MOTION WITH ACTION.

[Benjamin Franklin]

It is not what we do that counts, it is what we get done that
counts.

Ask yourself this question: Am I staying busy or am I
generating results?

We must keep on keeping on!

THE THOUGHTS OF THE RIGHTEOUS ARE RIGHT.

[Proverbs 12:5 - KJV]

Constantly fill your mind with positive affirmations. Every positive thought you put into your mind comes back multiplied.

Most people take a daily vitamin for their physical health. Many do not feed themselves mental vitamins.

YOU SET YOUR DESTINY BY WHAT YOU
MAKE OF YOURSELF. BE AN EARNEST
STUDENT OF YOURSELF. LEARN
BY FREQUENT SELF-EXAMINATION
TO APPRAISE AND IMPROVE YOUR
ATTITUDES, ASPIRATIONS, AND HABITS.

[Grenville Kleiser]

Greatness is never something conferred; it's always something
achieved. It's not given; it's earned. It's not an accident of
birth, but an attitude of quality – a dimension, an outlook, a
way of life that is open to anyone who is willing to pay the
price.

Talent is originality robed in resourcefulness. Achievement is
a dream dressed in work clothes. Accomplishment is ability
stripped of its doubts. Life is but a series of opportunities
masked as difficulties. Success is effort draped in day-to-day
self-improvement.

Never stop improving yourself.

LIVE ON THE RIGHT SIDE OF THE CONJUNCTION *"BUT"*.

One of the most profitable changes you can discipline yourself to make is to start living on the right side of the conjunction **"but."**

When we live on the wrong side of **"but,"** we say things like, *"Oh, I guess the meeting was OK, but it was too long."*

"I suppose I do have a lot to be grateful for, but I wish I didn't have all of this paperwork to complete."

Living on the right side of **"but"** means your reactions and attitudes are positive, affirmative, and optimistic!

On which side of the conjunction **"but"** are you living?

PERSONALITY CAN OPEN DOORS, BUT ONLY CHARACTER CAN KEEP THEM OPEN.

[Elmer G. Leterman]

Your Code of Ethics is a way of life that is intricately woven into your daily activities.

"The Revolver," a made-for-TV movie, tells the story of a young man who stopped some thieves snatching a lady's purse. Though he was a student and had no money, when the woman tried to pay him a reward, he wouldn't accept it. When asked why he wouldn't take the money, his explanation was simple, "There are some things that you do for the soul."

Do the right thing because doing the right thing is the right thing to do. This builds a spotless reputation, which is an invaluable asset.

Remember - there are some things you do for the soul!

34

ALL OF LIFE IS A RACE WITH UPS AND
DOWNS, AND ALL YOU HAVE TO DO TO
WIN THE RACE IS RISE EACH TIME YOU
FALL. "QUIT, GIVE UP, YOU'RE BEATEN,"
THEY STILL SHOUT IN YOUR FACE, BUT
A STRONGER VOICE INSIDE YOU SAYS,
"GET UP AND WIN THE RACE."

During the first four years after planting the Chinese bamboo
plant grows very little in height, even though it is watered
and fertilized regularly. Then, in the fifth year, after applying
water and fertilizer, the plant grows nearly ninety feet in
height in five weeks time!

The question: Did the Chinese bamboo tree grow ninety feet
in five weeks or in five years? The answer is that it grew
ninety feet in five years.

If at any time, the people had stopped watering and fertilizing,
the plant would have died. We are like this amazing plant; we
must continue to water and fertilize our life with hope, faith,
and perseverance, or we will die and leave our dreams to
wither away.

35

YOU CAN'T JUST TALK POSITIVE AND BE A
WINNER, YOU HAVE TO BELIEVE IT DEEP
INSIDE.

[Roger Staubach]

It's not enough to have the will to win, you need the will to
work to win. Here is a six-step procedure you can follow to
motivate yourself for the long haul:

- **Develop self-acceptance.** It is vital that you have a strong,
  healthy self-image.
- **Realize you have the potential for greatness.** Never
  entertain doubts about your ability to achieve greatness.
- **Plan for greatness.** Decide to do great things, then do all
  of the small things that add up to greatness.
- **Think like successful people think.** Ask yourself: "Is this
  the way a successful person would do it?"
- **Act as if it were impossible to fail.** Quiet confidence
  inspires others to want to see you succeed.
- **Monitor your results.** Studying the score causes the score
  to improve.

BE YOURSELF, BUT BE YOUR BEST SELF.

Bill Glass, the former Cleveland Browns All-Pro says to his audiences, "Be yourself, but learn to be your best self. Don't use being yourself as an excuse for laziness or mediocrity. Be what you ought to be. Stretch toward what you are created to be and in the stretching, you're certain to become a better and more effective person."

Measure your success by what you are, compared to what you **could** be.

Here are five guidelines for being at your best.

- **Know yourself.**
- **Believe in self-development.**
- **Be self-disciplined.**
- **Break your own record.**
- **Always bounce back.**

PEOPLE WHO ARE UNABLE TO MOTIVATE
THEMSELVES MUST BE CONTENT
WITH MEDIOCRITY, NO MATTER HOW
IMPRESSIVE THEIR OTHER TALENTS.

[Andrew Carnegie]

Enthusiasm is at the foundation of all progress! Enthusiasm is the difference between mediocrity and superior success in any endeavor.

Where do you get this energizing quality of enthusiasm and how do you maintain it?

1. **Take responsibility for your own level of enthusiasm throughout the day.** At the start of each new day, remind yourself of the good news: I have a high level of energy, a mind that is alert, challenging work, great potential, and a great future.

2. **Act as if you have enthusiasm even when you don't.** Enthusiasm reflects confidence, spreads good cheer, raises morale, inspires others, and generates loyalties. It draws people to you like a magnet. Enthusiasm is contagious.

BE ALERT FOR CHANCES TO EXPRESS
YOUR GRATITUDE TO THOSE WHO HAVE
HELPED OR EXTENDED A COURTESY OR
KINDNESS. IT WILL SET YOU APART.

[Bob Briner]

Here's an interesting illustration: In the fall of 1860, the steamship "Lady Elgin" set out with a total of 393 passengers and crew members to make the trip from Chicago to Milwaukee. Just off the shore of Evanston, she was rammed by a lumber schooner and sank. As a result, 279 of the passengers and crew died. Of those who were saved, 17 of them were saved by a student at Northwestern University, Edward W. Spence. He made 16 trips in all from the shore to the sinking ship and back again, saving the 17 lives.

Spence was in shock at the end of the 16th trip. It was reported that as they carried him to the hospital, he kept asking the question, "Did I do my best?" Edward Spence spent the remainder of his life as an invalid in a wheelchair.

In an interview with Chicago newspaper reporters, at 80 years of age, Edward Spence was asked, "What is your most vivid memory of that tragic fall day when the "Lady Elgin" went down off the coast of Evanston?" He replied, "The fact that not one of the 17 people whose lives I saved ever came back to say thank you – not one."

Look for opportunities to express appreciation. People want recognition as individuals more than any other single thing – even those who never perform a heroic act.

ONE MAN WITH COURAGE MAKES A MAJORITY.

[Andrew Jackson]

After Dr. David Livingstone had begun his now famous missionary work in Africa, a certain group wrote the great pioneer and asked: "Have you found a good road to where you are? If so, please advise. We'd like to send others to assist you."

Dr. Livingstone sent this reply: "If you have those who will come only if they know there is a good road, I don't want them. I want individuals who are strong and courageous – those who will come if there is no road at all!"

What a lesson in courage! Courage is performing the task that would be easier not to do. Courage is accepting the responsibilities when it would be more comfortable not to accept. It's moving out on faith, when you know full well the risks and the pitfalls that will challenge you. It's marching ahead, blazing a new trail where there are no roads, and sometimes no maps to guide you.

WATCH YOUR THOUGHTS, FOR THEY
BECOME WORDS. CHOOSE YOUR
WORDS, FOR THEY BECOME ACTIONS.
UNDERSTAND YOUR ACTIONS, FOR
THEY BECOME HABITS. STUDY YOUR
HABITS, FOR THEY WILL BECOME
YOUR CHARACTER. DEVELOP YOUR
CHARACTER, FOR IT BECOMES YOUR
DESTINY.

I AM . . .

- I am your constant companion.
- I am your greatest helper or your heaviest burden.
- I will push you onward or drag you down to failure.
- I am completely at your command.
- Half the things you do, you might as well turn them over to me and I will be able to do them quickly and correctly.
- I am easily managed; you must merely be firm with me.
- Show me exactly how you want something done and after a few lessons, I will do it automatically.
- Those who are great, I have made great.
- Those who are failures, I have made failures.
- I am not a machine, though I work with all the precision of a machine, plus the intelligence of a human being.
- Take me. Train me. Be firm with me and I will put the world at your feet.
- Be easy with me and I will destroy you.

I am . . . HABIT!

SUCCESSFUL PEOPLE FORM THE HABITS OF DOING THE THINGS FAILING PEOPLE DON'T LIKE TO DO.

[Albert E. N. Gray]

What would change your life if you were to do it consistently? Habits are choices repeated. Change your choices and you will change your life. Here are some habits you might want to adopt.

- Focus on the task at hand – do first things first.
- Finish what you start.
- Get up earlier - do something important.
- Stop taking work home.
- Become an expert.
- Go home earlier - spend more time with your family.
- Watch less TV.
- Go to bed earlier and get more rest.
- Eat less; exercise more.

According to some studies, it takes 21 days to change a habit. Why not think in terms of 30 days? If you can do something consistently for 30 days, you can do it forever. In a year, you could establish 12 new habits, one per month.

I HAVE FOUND IF YOU LOVE LIFE, LIFE WILL LOVE YOU BACK.

[Arthur Rubinstein]

According to the experts, there are seven steps to take if you wish to live longer, healthier days on earth.

1. **Stay active.**
2. **Be optimistic.**
3. **Cope with adversity.**
4. **Reduce your weight.**
5. **Plan significant events.**
6. **Change the pace.**
7. **Have periodic check-ups.**

Robust health and a high level of energy, keys to looking and feeling years younger, require more than following a set of rules. They also involve an optimistic, positive state of mind. Scientists are increasingly proving celebrated pianist Arthur Rubinstein was right when he said, *"I have found if you love life, life will love you back."* Rubinstein lived to be 95.

THE REWARDS OF WORKING HARD
WILL NOT GUARANTEE SUCCESS. BUT
YOU CAN'T BE SUCCESSFUL WITHOUT
WORKING HARD.

Develop a Code of Persistence.

Resolve to:

- Never give up so long as you know you are right.
- Believe all things will work out if you hang on until the end.
- Remain courageous and confident when the odds turn against you.
- Never permit anyone to intimidate you or shake your belief in yourself.
- Fight to overcome any physical handicaps and setbacks.
- Try again and again, and yet again, to reach your dreams.
- Take new faith and resolve from the knowledge that many successful men and women have had to fight defeat and adversity to achieve their greatness.

Success in life depends on your willingness to never give up. The reward is frequently delayed. Persistence is demanded.

44

DO WHAT YOU CAN, WITH WHAT YOU HAVE, WHERE YOU ARE.

[Theodore Roosevelt]

The "Acres of Diamonds" story is about a farmer who lived in Africa, at the time diamonds were discovered there. One day a friend told him of the millions being made by men who were discovering diamond mines. The farmer promptly sold his farm and left to search for diamonds himself. He searched all over the continent, but found no diamonds. As the story has it, finally penniless, in failing health and despondent, he threw himself into a river and drowned.

Long before this, the individual who had bought his farm found a large, unusual looking stone in the creek bed that ran through the farm. He placed it on his mantel. Enter here the same visitor who had told the original farmer about the diamond discoveries. He examined the stone and told the new owner that he had discovered one of the largest diamonds ever found - and that it was worth a fortune. To his surprise, the farmer told him the entire farm was covered with stones of that kind.

The first farmer had owned acres of diamonds but had made the mistake of not examining what he had before he ran off to something he hoped would prove to be better. For some, it may well be the grass is greener on the other side and they should move on. But, it is a good idea to examine what we have before we start looking somewhere else.

THE SECRET OF SUCCESS IS TO DO THE COMMON JOBS UNCOMMONLY WELL.

[John D. Rockefeller, Jr.]

Stamp it with excellence. There is an indescribable superiority added to the character and fiber of the people who consciously put the trademark of quality on their work. The mental and moral effect of doing things accurately, painstakingly and thoroughly can hardly be estimated because the processes are so gradual, so subtle.

Every time you obey the inward law of doing right, you hear an inward approval. On the contrary, every half completed, careless, slipshod job that goes out of your hands leaves its trace of demoralization behind, and excellence becomes impossible.

Whatever you do, give it your best - stamp it with excellence!

MY MOTHER TAUGHT ME VERY EARLY TO
BELIEVE I COULD ACCOMPLISH ANYTHING
I WANTED TO. THE FIRST WAS TO WALK
WITHOUT BRACES.

[Wilma Randolph - Three-time Olympic Gold Medalist]

Jean Henri Fabre conducted an experiment with processionary
caterpillars, so named because of their peculiar habit of
blindly following each other no matter how they are lined up or
where they are going.

This researcher took a group of these tiny creatures and
placed them in a circle. For 24 hours, the caterpillars dutifully
followed one another around and around. He then placed
the caterpillars on a round saucer full of pine needles (their
favorite food). For six days, the mindless creatures moved
around and around the saucer, literally dying of starvation
and exhaustion even though an abundance of choice food was
located less than two inches away.

The moral of this story: *You don't have to follow the crowd.*
Always look for other options.

NEARLY ALL MEN CAN STAND ADVERSITY, BUT IF YOU WANT TO TEST A MAN'S CHARACTER, GIVE HIM POWER.

[Abraham Lincoln]

Most of us perform well as we climb to the top. You should continue to perform well once you get there.

Abraham Lincoln taught me many things. This one-sentence philosophy stands at the top of the list of what I've learned from him.

48

YOUR MENTAL ATTITUDE GIVES YOUR
ENTIRE PERSONALITY A DRAWING POWER
THAT ATTRACTS THE CIRCUMSTANCES,
THINGS AND PEOPLE YOU THINK ABOUT
MOST!

Some people attract business, new customers and other
people as naturally as magnets attract particles of steel.
"They have the magic touch" you have heard it said of them.
If you analyze these people closely, you will find that they
have attractive qualities. So, what are these attractive
qualities?

- **Fine, cultivated manner** - They are able to do the right
  thing at the right time because they exercise common
  sense and good judgment.
- **Popular** - To be popular, you must strangle selfishness and
  you must learn to be polite, agreeable, and malleable.
- **Agreeable** - This will help you develop self-expression
  abilities like nothing else will. It will call out your success
  qualities and strengthen your empathy.
- **Frankness of manner** - Secretiveness and indecisiveness
  repel as much as frankness attracts.

Cultivate these attractive qualities.

THIS TIME, LIKE ALL TIMES, IS A VERY
GOOD TIME, IF WE BUT KNOW WHAT TO
DO WITH IT.

[Ralph Waldo Emerson]

Here are six Cs for effective daily living:

1. **Competence** - learn something new every day.

2. **Communication** - ask the right questions and you will get
   the right answers.

3. **Compassion** - make someone feel appreciated.

4. **Character** - always do right.

5. **Connection** - plant the seeds of relationships and nourish
   them with random acts of appreciation.

6. **Commitment -** be consistently committed to the above.

ONE OF THE BEST WAYS TO PERSUADE
OTHERS IS BY LISTENING TO THEM.

[Dean Rusk]

No matter what your station is in life, learn to listen. Develop
the habit of listening. We need to be good listeners, whether
in family matters or in our daily work.

THERE IS VERY LITTLE DIFFERENCE IN PEOPLE, BUT THAT LITTLE DIFFERENCE MAKES A BIG DIFFERENCE.

[W. Clement Stone]

Optimism is a way of thinking, not a feeling. Motivation tends to be based on how you feel about something. Optimism is based on how you think about a situation.

Optimism is the constant companion of high-performing people. It's their trademark, their way of life. Optimism is the difference that makes a big difference.

Learn to think optimistically. The result is energy. The result is eagerness to reach the next goal. The result is enthusiasm in your home. The result is success!

VIRTUE IS ITS OWN REWARD. THERE'S A PLEASURE IN DOING GOOD THAT SUFFICIENTLY PAYS ITSELF.

It's too bad we can't all read our obituaries and determine how other people view our life. The one exception was Alfred Nobel.

Nobel was the wealthy Swedish businessman who established the Nobel Prize. He had invented dynamite and became one of the world's largest producers of explosives. When his brother died in a test of explosives, a newspaper mistakenly printed Alfred's obituary instead of his brother's. It read:

"The Merchant of Death is dead ... Dr. Alfred Nobel, who became rich by finding ways to kill more people faster than ever before, died yesterday."

When Alfred read it and saw that his life amounted to so much destruction and killing, he was devastated. He decided to do something to benefit humanity, and he used his fortune to establish the Nobel Prize for people who do good in the world.

IRON RUSTS FROM DISUSE; STAGNANT WATER LOSES ITS PURITY AND IN COLD WEATHER BECOMES FROZEN; EVEN SO DOES INACTION SAP THE VIGOR OF THE MIND.

[Leonardo da Vinci]

Periodically you must step back and look at yourself. Are you satisfied with the human being you're becoming? How are you doing in your business? How are your personal relationships? Are you moving forward? Are you getting better? Are you using your time effectively?

All of us are aware of situations where people fall by the wayside - they drop out. They stop learning. They stop growing. They stop getting better. It's at this precise point they compromise what they will become as human beings. They expect others to grow and get better. However, all too often, these people make the assumption that they are good enough to meet the challenges and changes of the future without improving themselves.

Remind yourself to keep growing. Keep learning and studying. Periodically, step back and take a look!

CHANGE IS THE LAW OF LIFE. THOSE WHO LOOK ONLY TO THE PAST OR THE PRESENT ARE CERTAIN TO MISS THE FUTURE.

[John F. Kennedy]

In a most interesting study, an economist condensed 50,000 years of recorded history into just 50 years.

In this distilled version of history, it was only 10 years ago that you and I emerged from the cave. The first 40 years meant practically nothing in the way of progress. Just 2 years ago Christ walked along the shores of the Sea of Galilee. Ten months ago Gutenberg invented the printing press. Ten days ago Edison discovered electricity. On that same day, Sheldon fathered salesmanship. Last week, the Wright Brothers made that first successful airplane ride. Five days ago someone pushed a button and you heard your first radio broadcast from KDKA in Pittsburgh. Late yesterday another button was pushed and you viewed television for the first time. It was a matter of minutes ago that the first jet broke the sound barrier. Only a few seconds later, Armstrong landed on the moon . . .

You are probably facing a change today that if viewed properly, will bring about growth and even more success.

THERE ARE TWO KINDS OF PEOPLE IN
THE WORLD: THOSE WHO ARE ALWAYS
GETTING READY TO DO SOMETHING, AND
THOSE WHO GO AHEAD AND DO IT.

Show up on time, dressed, ready to play.

I learned this from Dr. Michael Mescon. Here's the way he
dramatizes it: "If you just show up you're going to have 75% of
the people in this world beat. If you show up on time, now you
have 90% of the people beat. If you show up on time, dressed,
ready to play, you'll have them all beat. That's the way to be
successful."

That's what he would tell his young students getting ready to
go out into the business world. That's the way you become
highly successful.

WORK EXPANDS SO AS TO FILL THE TIME AVAILABLE FOR ITS COMPLETION.

[C. Northcote Parkinson - Parkinson's Law]

Fred Smith, a mentor and friend of mind, taught many things in his lifetime. He taught me to always give people more than they can do and they will find a way to get it done.

WHAT MOTIVATES PEOPLE IS WHAT MOTIVATES PEOPLE.

Motivation is a difficult concept for most people. Suppose you have two excellent people. You would like to reward one with a raise in pay, but money, it turns out, is not an issue with this person since his spouse has a good job that provides a nice second income. He may see increased responsibility as an appropriate reward.

On the other hand, you would like to reward the second person with more responsibility, but her spouse's unexpected illness has created big medical bills. For this person, money is a greater motivator than increased responsibility.

How do you know what motivation works with what people? Ask! Try something like, "If you perform well, what reward or recognition could you receive that would make you want to continue to perform at a high level?" It pays to ask this important question. Try asking your children this question!

[Excerpt from The Heart of a Leader, Ken Blanchard]

IT'S MORE IMPORTANT AS A MANAGER TO BE RESPECTED THAN TO BE POPULAR.

[Ken Blanchard and Don Shula - Everyone's a Coach]

Think back to a leader you had – a parent, teacher, coach or boss who got great performance from you. More than likely, this leader combined toughness and kindness. You knew that person cared about you, but that he or she would not let up on you in the quest for excellence.

If you, as a leader, demand that your people add value to the organization through their work, you must fulfill your end of the bargain by telling the truth and keeping work standards high. This often means sacrificing popularity in your endeavor to do the right thing.

Are you willing to push your people beyond their comfort zone in order to achieve excellence? They might not like what you ask of them, but they will remember you as a leader they respected.

LEADERSHIP IS INFLUENCE. THAT'S IT – NOTHING MORE, NOTHING LESS.

[John Maxwell]

According to this definition, we are all leaders on some level. Whether you are leading a family, an organization, a little league sports team, a committee, a business, or a multi-million dollar enterprise – you influence others.

Rick Loy suggests there are five traits you must have if you want to be a positive influence. The next five vitamins will deal with the traits you need to develop to become a positive influence.

Trait #1

EXCELLENT CHARACTER

[Rick Loy - Sales Vice President - AdvoCare International]

Your character arrives before you do and stays long after you're gone.

Trait #2

EXEMPLARY CONDUCT

[Rick Loy - Sales Vice President - AdvoCare International]

You want to make sure that your walk matches your talk.

Trait #3

ENCOURAGING CONVERSATION

[Rick Loy - Sales Vice President - AdvoCare International]

Most everyone you come in contact with, every day, needs encouragement.

Trait #4

EXCEPTIONAL COMPETENCY

[Rick Loy - Sales Vice President - AdvoCare International]

You improve your competence by gaining knowledge and
constantly improving skills. The by-product is confidence.

Trait #5

EXPANDING CONTRIBUTIONS

[Rick Loy - Sales Vice President - AdvoCare International]

Always do more than you are paid to do. Go the extra mile; it has few traffic jams.

65

THE GREATEST DISCOVERY OF MY
GENERATION IS THAT PEOPLE CAN
CHANGE THEIR LIVES BY CHANGING
THEIR ATTITUDES.

[William James]

Keep your mind positive. Stay optimistic in everything you do.
Always look on the brighter side. Stay away from negative
people; stay close to those who are honest and upbeat.

TRYING IS JUST A NOISY WAY OF NOT DOING SOMETHING.

Author and consultant, Art Turock, teaches that we need to make a distinction between being interested and being committed. When you are "interested" in doing something, you only do it when it's convenient, but when you are "committed," you follow through no matter what – no excuses!

Many people are interested rather than committed. They talk about trying to do something, rather than actually doing it. They make lots of noise, but fail to follow up. An interested exerciser wakes up in the morning to rain and says, "I think I'll exercise tomorrow." A committed exerciser wakes up to rain and says, "I better exercise inside."

When a person is committed to doing something, he or she will find ways to suppress rationalization. Even when it is inconvenient, such a person will keep his or her commitment. Persistence in life is characterized by this mental and behavioral toughness.

[Excerpt from The Heart of a Leader, Ken Blanchard]

HIGH ACHIEVERS IN ALL FIELDS UNDERSTAND THE POWER OF THE MADE-UP MIND. THEY THINK RIGHT.

Dr. Edward Rosenow, a renowned surgeon at Mayo Clinic, established his purpose in life and sealed his commitment to medicine when he was just a young boy living in Minnesota's northwoods country. One night, he says, his younger brother became quite ill, and the family gathered together, waiting nervously until a doctor could be located.

When a doctor finally arrived and examined the sick boy, young Edward's eyes were riveted on the anguished faces of his parents. At last, the doctor looked up, turned to the parents, and said, "You folks can relax now. Your boy is going to be all right."

Edward Rosenow, then just eleven, was so impressed with the change the doctor's words brought to his parents' faces that he said, "I resolved right then that one day I would become a doctor, so I could spend my life putting that same light in other people's faces."

Never underestimate the power of the made-up mind.

TALK DOES NOT COOK RICE.

[Chinese Proverb]

I have always liked the old cliché, actions speak louder than words.

The Bible says, ". . . by their fruits you shall know them."

PLAN TO WAKE UP EMPLOYED.

[Jack and Garry Kinder]

Always plan your work the day before on a clean sheet of paper. Put down everything that needs to be done. Then go back and prioritize what's most important so that you do first things first.

YOU WILL BE THE SAME PERSON IN FIVE
YEARS THAT YOU ARE TODAY EXCEPT
FOR TWO THINGS: THE PEOPLE YOU
MEET AND THE BOOKS YOU READ.

[Charlie Tremendous Jones]

Here are four success-proven guideposts that will lead you to greater achievements and enrich your mind.

- **Read.** Setting aside just 15 minutes a day will enable you to read up to two dozen books a year. Keep it up and you'll have read 1,000 books in your lifetime. That's the equivalent of going through college five times.
- **Mark.** The riches of reading will rapidly multiply for you as you mark, underline, challenge, and often editorialize in the margins.
- **Learn.** To learn is to understand, to comprehend, or to attain proficiency in a subject. One of the most effective ways of learning is to outline the book.
- **Inwardly Digest.** It's not only what individuals eat, but also what they digest, that gives them strength. Likewise, it's not only what we read and how much we read, but what we "digest," what we "internalize," that adds to our knowledge and understanding.

Learn the riches of reading – and in turn you can enrich the lives of your associates and your family!

IT'S NOT THE WAY THE WIND BLOWS, IT'S HOW YOU SET YOUR SAILS.

You and only you decide where you are going to go. It is not up to your Grandpa or Grandma.

When the sail is properly set, this means you are getting the most power out of the wind.

Once you determine the direction you want to go, immediately head in that direction. You may have to "sail" into the wind.

A MAN'S PRIDE SHALL BRING HIM LOW:
BUT HONOUR SHALL UPHOLD THE
HUMBLE IN SPIRIT.

[Proverbs 29:23 - KJV]

Be thankful for your abilities. Give glory to God and others.

There is a fine line between confidence and arrogance – be
sure you recognize the difference.

Always be humble in victory and courageous in defeat. In
victories great and small, be thankful, giving credit to others
for their contributions. In defeat, accept responsibility, make
necessary corrections, and move forward.

WHEN YOU REACH THE END OF YOUR ROPE, TIE A KNOT AND HANG ON!

[Cyrus Hall]

A solid base for success is perseverance. Dismissed from a major newspaper with the advice to try something else because he had no talent, a young man considered giving up – but he didn't. His name ... Walt Disney.

Another young man who loved flying crash-landed the first two times he soloed, and the third time he flew head-on into another aircraft. Give up? Not Admiral Richard Byrd!

Author Rod Serling of Twilight Zone fame, wrote and tried to market 40 stories before he sold one.

The great triumphs of your life will be the rewards of your persistence. Never depend on your genius to carry you. If you have talent, improve it. If you have none, develop it, but do not depend on it.

Perseverance, not genius, separates winners from losers. Never give up!

WHEN WORK IS A PLEASURE, LIFE IS A
JOY. WHEN WORK IS A DUTY, LIFE IS
SLAVERY.

[Maxim Gorky - Russian Novelist]

Often the difference between experiencing work as pleasure
and work as duty lies in how we look at it.

That is the point of the popular parable from medieval times
that tells of a traveler journeying through Italy. He comes
upon three stonecutters who are sweating and toiling under a
glaring, hot, afternoon sun. The traveler asks the first man:
"What are you doing?" He replies, *"I am cutting a stone."*
Turning to the second man, the traveler asks: *"What are you
doing?"* The second stonecutter replies: *"I'm earning 100
lira per day."* When asked this question the third stonecutter
responded, *"I am building a beautiful cathedral that will last
for centuries!"*

Ask yourself three important questions:
1. How do I view work in general?
2. How do I view my specific work?
3. How do I view myself as a worker?

See yourself adding value to your community and creating
something of long standing benefit to others.

FINALLY, BRETHREN, WHATSOEVER
THINGS ARE TRUE, WHATSOEVER THINGS
ARE HONEST, WHATSOEVER THINGS ARE
JUST, WHATSOEVER THINGS ARE PURE,
WHATSOEVER THINGS ARE LOVELY,
WHATSOEVER THINGS ARE OF GOOD
REPORT; IF THERE BE ANY VIRTUE, AND
IF THERE BE ANY PRAISE, THINK ON
THESE THINGS.

[Philippians 4:8 - KJV]

Change your thoughts; change your life.

When you begin focusing on the positive aspects of life, even if
your circumstances do not change, you will find you are better
equipped to handle whatever comes your way.

Think on the good things. Thank God for family, for friends, for
health.

NEVER TAKE COUNSEL OF YOUR FEARS.

Always be looking for inspiration from reading, from friends, from God.

Inspiration and enthusiasm are contagious. Why don't you start an epidemic today!

WHEN I STAND BEFORE GOD AT THE
END OF MY LIFE, I WOULD HOPE THAT
I WOULD NOT HAVE A SINGLE BIT OF
TALENT LEFT AND COULD SAY, "I USED
EVERYTHING YOU GAVE ME."

[Erma Bombeck]

Life is short and life is fragile.

You never know what a day may bring. That's reason enough
to be at your best every day! Live every moment to the fullest.

I EXPECT TO PASS THROUGH THIS LIFE
BUT ONCE. THEREFORE, IF THERE BE
ANY KINDNESS I CAN SHOW, OR ANY
GOOD THING I CAN DO FOR ANOTHER
HUMAN BEING, LET ME DO IT NOW, FOR I
SHALL NOT PASS THIS WAY AGAIN.

[Stephen Grellet]

Kindness and goodness never go out of style.

Opportunities to show kindness by doing good deeds are
abundant. Just take a look around. You don't have to look far
– but do look!

THE HAND OF THE DILIGENT SHALL BEAR
RULE: BUT THE SLOTHFUL SHALL BE
UNDER TRIBUTE.

[Proverbs 12:24 - KJV]

Working hard will not guarantee success.

But you cannot be successful without working hard.

PERHAPS THE MOST VALUABLE RESULT
OF ALL EDUCATION IS THE ABILITY TO
MAKE YOURSELF DO THE THING YOU
HAVE TO DO, WHEN IT OUGHT TO BE
DONE, WHETHER YOU LIKE DOING IT OR
NOT.

[Thomas Huxley]

Nicholas Murray Butler, former Chancellor of Columbia University, once said, "There are three kinds of people in the world today – those who make things happen, those who watch things happen, and those who have no idea of what is happening. Distinguish yourself by having the ability to make things happen."

People who enjoy the reputation of knowing how to get a job done tell me the secret lies in forcing yourself to take that first step toward achieving some kind of victory today.

Don't wonder or ponder or contemplate too long. Don't wait until you feel like it. Don't wait until conditions are just right, instead, "begin it!"

THE GREATEST SATISFACTION IN THE WORLD IS WORK WELL DONE.

[J.C. Penney]

The late Earl Nightingale sent me some definitions one time called, *"The Greatest Things."* I review them often to help me remember just what's important and what isn't.

- The best day, *today.*
- The greatest puzzle, *life.*
- The best policy, *honesty.*
- The greatest thought, *God.*
- The greatest mystery, *death.*
- The best work, work you *like.*
- The greatest mistake, *giving up.*
- The most ridiculous asset, *pride.*
- The greatest need, *common sense.*
- The most dangerous person, *a liar.*
- The best advice, use *good manners.*
- The wisest short-cut, *develop mentors.*
- The greatest fault, *to be aware of none.*
- The greatest truth, *we reap what we sow.*
- The most expensive indulgence, *self-pity.*
- The greatest deceiver, *one who deceives self.*
- The best habit, *making good on all commitments.*
- The best teacher, *one who brings out the best in you.*
- The saddest feeling, *feeling envious of another's success.*
- The greatest thing in the world, *love* - love of family, home, friends, associates, company and country.

WHAT YOU DO WHEN YOU DON'T HAVE TO, DETERMINES EXACTLY WHAT YOU'LL BE WHEN YOU CAN NO LONGER HELP IT.

[Jack Murray]

The difference between star performers and mediocre performers is about five minutes. The stars spend five minutes more in planning and preparation. They invest five minutes more in research and study. They are self-disciplined and this quality makes the difference.

Disciplined star performers are:
- Enthusiastic
- Resourceful
- Predictable
- Dependable
- Courageous
- Persistent
- Optimistic
- Dedicated

Continue to develop the five-minute difference – self-discipline!

THE FIRST THING TO DO, IF YOU HAVE
NOT DONE IT, IS TO FALL IN LOVE WITH
YOUR WORK.

[Henry Ward Beecher]

Peak performers are those individuals who manage to go to the
top and stay there. Peak performers have these four common
characteristics:

- **Pay Attention** – They don't just look, they see something.
  They don't just listen, they hear something.
- **Pay The Price** – They have a passion to excel. No price is
  too great. Peak Performers focus. They consistently do the
  things their competitors will not or cannot do.
- **Are Promoters** – They become known for what they
  know. They find ways to distinguish themselves from the
  competition.
- **Persist** – They believe in the type of philosophy advanced
  by Cyrus Hall at Hallmark Cards, *"When you reach the end
  of your rope, tie a knot and hang on."*

OUTDISTANCE THE COMPETITION BY OUT-SERVING THE COMPETITION.

To outdistance your competition you must learn more and better ways to out-serve them. You do this by consistently doing the right thing, in the right way, at the right time, and always in the best interest of other people - those you serve.

Out-serve the competition by demonstrating a genuine interest in your clients, their problems, their concerns and their aspirations.

Frank Leahy said, *"Learn from others. Strive to be a perfectionist. Believe in over-compensation. Never follow the line of least resistance. Practice the correct way, not the easy way. These attitudes overcome the opposition and bring victory."*

YOU MANAGE THINGS; YOU LEAD PEOPLE.

[Captain Grace Hopper]

You use the computer to crunch numbers, but don't crunch the people.

In tough times, whether it is a war or everyday life, you can't manage the people into battle; you must lead them into battle.

You lead by example. Follow a set of standards and live by ethical principles. This invokes respect from others and develops loyalty.

If you look around and there isn't anybody following you – you are not the leader!

TO LOVE IS TO PLACE OTHERS BEFORE YOU AND TO MAKE THEIR NEEDS YOUR PRIORITY. DO IT.

[Tony Snow]

118th Annual Commencement Address: "Reason, Faith, Vocation"
Tony Snow, White House Press Secretary
Basilica of the National Shrine of Immaculate Conception
May 12, 2007

When you put somebody else at the center of the frame, your entire world changes, and for the better.

You begin to find your own place in the world. When you're drawn into the lives of others, you enter their problems, their hopes, their dreams, their families. They whisk you down unimagined corridors, toward possibilities that had been hidden to you before. So resolve to do little things for others.

If you engage them with heart and mind, with faith and energy, you are going to find yourself on a cresting wave. It'll carry you forward and it'll push you under water from time to time. And some day in the dim and distant future, when you're looking back at it, you're not going to think about your car or your career or your gold watch. You'll think about a chewed-up teddy bear you had as a baby or maybe your child's smile on a special Christmas morning. The only things that are sure to endure are the artifacts of love. So go out and build as many as you can.

THE SECRET OF SUCCESS IS THAT THERE IS NO SECRET – THAT IS THE SECRET.

[Jack and Garry Kinder]

You become successful by following systems that work and philosophies that win on a daily basis.

You continually improve the systems. You add to the systems.

On the other hand, principles and philosophies rarely, if ever, change. You may add to them, but you rarely change them.

COURAGE IS CONTAGIOUS. WHEN A
BRAVE PERSON TAKES THE STAND, THE
SPINES OF OTHERS ARE STIFFENED.

[Billy Graham]

Know what you believe about the important things in life.
Know what you stand for, then stand for it; others will be
inspired by your courage.

TAKE RESPONSIBILITY FOR MAKING RELATIONSHIPS WORK.

Here's a question to ask yourself about all your relationships – personal and business: Do you want the relationship to work? If so, then you must take personal responsibility for making it work. And forget the word "trying." Trying is just a noisier way of not doing something.

I know a couple who have been married for twenty-five years. They are an inspiration to others. Whenever they see each other they both light up with joy. It's obvious that they're best friends. It's easy to accentuate the negative, but these two do everything they can to point out the positive and bring out the best in each other. They are both committed to doing whatever it takes to show respect and unconditional appreciation.

In short, they are committed to making their relationship work. That's what it takes these days in all types of relationships – personal and professional.

[Excerpt from The Heart of a Leader, Ken Blanchard]

THERE IS AN ART IN SILENCE, AND
THERE IS AN ELOQUENCE IN IT, TOO.

[Ken Blanchard]

Being a good listener is a forgotten art that is simply magic.
Show people you are sincerely interested in what they are
saying; give them all the eager attention and appreciation that
they crave and are so hungry for, but seldom get.

Here's how you can develop the art of listening:

- Look people straight in the eyes when they are talking.
- Give them your undivided attention. This communicates
  that you think what they have to say is important.
- Listen to what people are actually saying.
- When you really listen, it makes any questions you ask
  more productive; you will uncover what they are not saying.
- When you uncover what they are not saying, you have
  helped them discover what they needed to say, but didn't
  know how.

Become a good listener.

YOU HAD BETTER LIVE YOUR BEST, THINK
YOUR BEST AND DO YOUR BEST TODAY
- FOR TODAY WILL SOON BE TOMORROW
AND TOMORROW WILL SOON BE FOREVER.

Winners establish and maintain their momentum. It's like
starting a locomotive. It takes 238 pounds of pressure to get
a locomotive started. It only takes 33 pounds to keep the
locomotive travelling once it has gained full speed. But if the
locomotive stops, it takes 238 pounds of pressure to get it
started again.

Once you get rolling, it only takes a small amount of effort
to keep rolling. If you stop or have an interruption in your
activity, it takes the same amount of discipline and effort to
reestablish the momentum that it did at the very beginning.
The key to momentum is to build a winning tradition. Most any
team can get "up" to win one game, but the secret is to get
"up" consistently.

Momentum comes to professionals who have the tenacity to
stick it out when the going gets tough. When they have a job
to do and see their goal clearly and take all the hard knocks in
stride, they power through all problems and obstacles.

2nd
QUARTER

The first five days of this 2nd quarter I bring you five mental vitamins from the great Paul Meyer. These vitamins are what Paul called his Personal Million Dollar Success Plan.

Paul Meyer taught me that we are all salespeople in life and in livelihood. Being able to sell yourself or your brand brings increased business, regardless of your profession. That's the underlying philosophy in his writings.

Used with permission from The Meyer Resource Group.

Step #1

CRYSTALLIZE YOUR THINKING.

[Paul J. Meyer - Step 1 - The Million-Dollar Personal Success Plan]

Determine what specific goal you want to achieve. Then
dedicate yourself to its attainment with unswerving singleness of
purpose, the trenchant zeal of a crusader.

93

Step #2

DEVELOP A PLAN FOR ACHIEVING
YOUR GOAL, AND A DEADLINE FOR ITS
ATTAINMENT.

[Paul J. Meyer - Step 2 - The Million-Dollar Personal Success Plan]

Plan your progress carefully: hour by hour, day by day, month
by month. Organized activity and enthusiasm are the wellsprings
of your power.

Step #3

DEVELOP A SINCERE DESIRE FOR THE THINGS YOU WANT IN LIFE.

[Paul J. Meyer - Step 3 - The Million-Dollar Personal Success Plan]

A burning desire is the greatest motivator of every human action. The desire for success implants "success consciousness," which in turn creates a vigorous and ever-increasing "habit of success."

Step #4

DEVELOP SUPREME CONFIDENCE IN
YOURSELF AND YOUR OWN ABILITIES.

[Paul J. Meyer - Step 4 - The Million-Dollar Personal Success Plan]

Enter every activity without giving mental recognition to the
possibility of defeat. Concentrate on your strengths, instead of
your weaknesses ... on your powers, instead of your problems.

Step #5

DEVELOP A DOGGED DETERMINATION
TO FOLLOW THROUGH ON YOUR PLAN,
REGARDLESS OF OBSTACLES, CRITICISM
OR CIRCUMSTANCES OR WHAT OTHER
PEOPLE SAY, THINK OR DO.

[Paul J. Meyer - Step 5 - The Million-Dollar Personal Success Plan]

Opportunities never come to those who wait; they are captured
by those who dare to attack.

THE TRUTH OF THE MATTER IS THAT YOU ALWAYS KNOW THE RIGHT THING TO DO. THE HARD PART IS DOING IT.

[Gen. Norman Schwarzkopf]

Most all of us know the best thing to do. The tough part is execution. Ask yourself frequently, what is my number one priority right now? Then, remember what W. Clement Stone taught us, "Do it now!"

MAKE PRIORITIZING A PRIORITY.

[Howard Wight]

On a daily basis, develop a written Master Action Plan (MAP).
Your daily priorities should dovetail with your lifetime goals.

PUT ENTHUSIASM TO WORK.

Develop your slight edge:

- Show that you care – by attitude, word, and action.
- Treat others as you would like to be treated.
- Respect others' intelligence.
- Do today's jobs today – never put off until tomorrow.
- Make right first impressions.
- Seek answers to unanswered questions; admit when you don't know.
- Deliver more than is expected.
- Encourage others with your enthusiasm to make sure the job is well done, and done right.

I WILL GREET THIS DAY WITH LOVE IN MY HEART.

[Og Mandino - Scroll #II The Greatest Salesman in the World]

"Mandino wrote, love is the single most important quality for success. Love can increase sales and bring about all the skills and knowledge of the world. I will look on all things with love and I will be born again. I will love the sun for it warms my bones, yet I will love the rain for it cleanses my spirit. I will love the light for it shows me the way, yet I will love the darkness for it shows me the stars."

HE THAT WALKETH WITH WISE MEN SHALL BE WISE.

[Proverbs 13:20 - KJV]

Associate with good people and you'll keep getting better and better all the time.

Surround yourself with people who are successfully doing the things you want to do. Seek out a mentor – become a mentor.

102

SEE YOURSELF WINNING. YOUR SELF-
IMAGE HAS TO BE STRONG, POSITIVE
AND OPTIMISTIC BEFORE YOU GET TO
THE TOP.

[Dennis Conner]

Developing confidence is the first principle of professionalism.
Why? Because confidence in yourself will create the same
feeling in others. Here are seven simple ways in which you
can develop this all-important confidence.

1. **Build Your Appearance.** Appearance affects attitudes
   - yours as well as your prospect's. Be aware of your
   posture. Project a professional presence.
2. **Act the Part.** Whatever it is that you would like to do
   better, act as though you are already good at it.
3. **Speak Faster.** Make a habit of increasing your rate of
   speech and take note of its impact on others. Immediately,
   you will appear and feel more enthusiastic and confident.
4. **Compete, But Don't Compare.** Build your own "game
   plan." Compare your life with what you ought to be.
5. **Practice What You Do Well.** Confidence flows best from
   successful experiences. Build on your strengths.
6. **Cooperate with Life.** Focus your attentions and energies
   on those things you can do something about.
7. **Develop a Mentor.** Find someone who will be genuinely
   interested in your success.

WHEN PEOPLE STOP GETTING BETTER, THEY CEASE TO BE GOOD.

The person who decides to coast is going to coast downhill. You can't coast the bicycle uphill. So the moment you decide to coast in any area of life, you're going downhill.

It's okay to retire. In today's world, people should retire and stay active. Some will go into another business. Some will get active in a charity. Stay active, keep your mind alert.

104

AS AN EARRING OF GOLD, AND AN ORNAMENT OF FINE GOLD, SO IS A WISE REPROVER UPON AN OBEDIENT EAR.

[Proverbs 25:12 - KJV]

Over and over again the Bible teaches us to accept valid criticism. Surround yourself with friends who will tell you quickly and honestly where you have gotten off the path or missed a step.

THE SECRET OF JOY IN WORK IS CONTAINED IN ONE WORD – EXCELLENCE. TO KNOW HOW TO DO SOMETHING WELL IS TO ENJOY IT.

[Pearl S. Buck]

Don't expect perfection – expect excellence.

There's a big difference in the results you get from expecting perfection and expecting excellence.

Expecting perfection paralyzes people. They become afraid to do anything at all for fear of failure. The result is a lot of activity, no results.

Don't expect perfection from yourself. Don't expect perfection from your associates. Expect excellence. Expect them to do their best. If they always strive to be at their best, the results will take care of themselves.

DON'T WAIT UNTIL PEOPLE DO THINGS EXACTLY RIGHT BEFORE YOU PRAISE THEM.

[Ken Blanchard and Spencer Johnson - The One Minute Manager]

Many well-intentioned people wait to praise others until they do things exactly right – complete the project or accomplish the goal. The problem here is that they could wait forever. You see, "exactly right" behavior is made up of a whole series of approximately right behaviors. It makes more sense to praise progress – it's a moving target.

Can you imagine standing a child up and saying, "Walk," and when he falls down, you say, "I told you to walk!" and then spanking him. Of course not! You stand the child up and he wobbles a bit. You shout, "You stood!" and shower him with hugs and kisses. The next day, he wobbles a step and you are all over him with praise. Gradually, the child gains confidence until he finally walks. It's the same with adults. Catch them doing things right – and in the beginning approximately right is fine.

GREAT PERFORMERS DO NOT WAIT FOR INSPIRATION.

Great performers get up and get the job done. Here are two examples – Winston Churchill and Abraham Lincoln. They have been called by many people the greatest leaders of the last 500 years. Dr. Billy Graham says, "They're the two greatest leaders since the Apostle Paul."

Both of them fought serious depression every day of their lives. Both of them spoke with clarity, and both of them kept it simple. They didn't wait for inspiration; they just got up every day and got the job done.

At 80, late in his life, Churchill made this observation, "I have noticed that people getting the job done in this world are people that don't feel good."

If you get into action, you'll feel better. Understand that feelings always follow actions.

LOVE NEVER DIVIDES; IT ALWAYS MULTIPLIES.

[Dr. W. A. Criswell]

When my wife, Janet, and I were talking with Dr. Criswell before our wedding, he gave us this sage advice about a second marriage. He said, "Your love for one person will never diminish your love for another." He was talking about our deceased spouses. He wisely counseled us, "Love never divides; it always multiplies. What this world needs is more love."

Jesus was once asked by a lawyer what was the greatest commandment. "Jesus said unto him, 'Thou shalt love the Lord thy God with all thy heart, and with all thy soul, and with all thy mind.' This is the first and great commandment. And the second is like unto it, Thou shalt love thy neighbour as thyself. On these two commandments hang all the law and the prophets" (Matthew 22:37-40).

TRY NOT TO BE A PERSON OF SUCCESS BUT RATHER A PERSON OF VALUE.

[Albert Einstein]

You want to know in your own heart that every day you're doing God's will.

You want to be viewed as a person of value in the eyes of God rather than being what the world calls successful.

A MIND TROUBLED BY DOUBT CANNOT FOCUS ON THE COURSE TO VICTORY.

[Arthur Golden]

Know what you want to get done. Go for it with everything you have, every day.

Tentative action brings about tentative results.

THE ART OF BEING WISE IS KNOWING WHAT TO OVERLOOK.

[William James]

Don't get caught up in small things. Get involved in the big things of life.

Stop worrying about things you can't control and get your eyes focused on the things you can control.

WITH ALL THY GETTING, GET GOING.

In Proverbs 4:7, we read, "Wisdom is the principal thing; therefore, get wisdom. And with all thy getting, get understanding."

Jesus taught with all thy getting, get going. Go into the world. Go, sin no more. Go in peace. Go spread my teachings.

CHARACTER IS LIKE A TREE AND
REPUTATION IS LIKE A SHADOW. THE
SHADOW IS WHAT WE THINK OF IT; THE
TREE IS THE REAL THING.

[Abraham Lincoln]

Keep your eyes on the real thing; like Lincoln, you'll leave a
long shadow.

THE SUPERIOR PERSON IS MODEST IN SPEECH, BUT EXCEEDS IN ACTIONS.

[Confucius]

The Bible tells us to be slow to speak, slow to anger and quick to listen.

Actions speak louder than words.

CHARACTER IS THE INTEGRITY TO
FOLLOW THROUGH ON A RESOLUTION
LONG AFTER A MOMENT OF MOTIVATION
HAS PASSED.

Making a commitment is easy; keeping a commitment is hard.

Make up your mind to follow through on all commitments, even
when nobody is watching.

116

I TALK AND TALK AND TALK, AND I
HAVEN'T TAUGHT PEOPLE IN 50 YEARS
WHAT MY FATHER TAUGHT ME BY
EXAMPLE IN ONE WEEK.

[Mario Cuomo]

People would rather see a sermon than hear one any day.
They'd rather one should walk with them than merely show the
way. Fine counsel can be confusing, but exampie's always
clear.

I learned from this poem by Edgar Guest that people would
rather see a sermon than hear one any day.

117

PROFESSIONALS KNOW THEY ARE GOOD,
AND THEY KNOW WHY THEY ARE GOOD.

Focus on what makes you good. Get better and better. Learn and study. Record your performance. Grow!

Good professionals are those who have confidence in themselves and their abilities.

Great professionals are those whose associates have confidence in them and their abilities.

COMPETE BUT DON'T COMPARE.

You set goals so that you can compete with others, but not to compare yourself to others. You compare yourself to what you ought to be.

Geoffrey Gabrino said the real contest is always between what you've done and what you're capable of doing. You measure yourself against yourself and nobody else.

WHAT WE'VE DONE FOR OURSELVES
ALONE DIES WITH US; WHAT WE'VE DONE
FOR OTHERS AND THE WORLD REMAINS,
AND IS IMMORTAL.

[Albert Pike]

Try to always get caught up in something bigger than you
are. Get involved in the needs of others and your needs will
disappear.

SUCCESS CONSISTS OF GOING FROM
FAILURE TO FAILURE WITHOUT A LOSS
OF ENTHUSIASM.

[Sir Winston Churchill]

General George Patton taught that the true measure of people
is how they bounce when they hit bottom.

Everybody goes through some tough times. Churchill says go
through those tough times without the loss of enthusiasm.

WHAT THE MIND CAN CONCEIVE AND
BELIEVE, WITH THE GRACE OF GOD, THE
MIND CAN ACHIEVE.

[Napoleon Hill]

Robert L. Schwartz said, "The entrepreneur is essentially
a visualizer and an actualizer. Entrepreneurs visualize
something, and when they visualize it they see exactly how to
make it happen."

122

IN ALL THY WAYS ACKNOWLEDGE HIM,
AND HE SHALL DIRECT THY PATHS.

[Proverbs 3:6 - KJV]

In everything you do, put God first, others second and
yourself third. He will keep you on the path, and on the path,
going in the right direction.

THINK BIG! ACT BIG! BE BIG!

[Norman Vincent Peale]

At his ninetieth birthday party, Norman Vincent Peale, the great minister of positive thinking, shared a story about a man he met on an airplane. The man looked worried so Norman decided to engage him in conversation. "What's wrong?" he asked. After some coaxing, the man shared that he had just received a promotion, but had doubts about whether he had what it would take to handle the job.

"Yes you do!" stated Dr. Peale. "How do you know?" the man replied. Dr. Peale answered, "You do if you think you do." Then he encouraged the man to start each day by chanting, "Think big! Act big! Be big!" By the time they landed, the man was in a different frame of mind.

Be your own best friend and believe in yourself. Don't wait for someone to do it for you. Cheer yourself on. Write your own pep talk. It works.

[Excerpt from The Heart of a Leader. Ken Blanchard]

RULE YOUR MIND OR YOUR MIND WILL RULE YOU.

[Horace]

Take your mental vitamins. Feed your mind as you'd feed your body.

Our minds are like a computer – what goes in is what comes out.

NOBODY EVER GAVE THEIR BEST AND
REGRETTED IT.

[George Ellis]

Be at your best every day. Strive for excellence in every area.
You may not always win, but you have the sure knowledge that
you did your best every day.

126

I AM MORE AFRAID OF AN ARMY OF 100
SHEEP LED BY A LION THAN AN ARMY OF
100 LIONS LED BY A SHEEP.

[Talleyrand]

Everybody is a leader, whether it's in family life, spiritual life
or your daily work.

Lead like a lion – know where you are going and be
courageous.

I CANNOT DO EVERYTHING, BUT I CAN DO SOMETHING. I MUST NOT FAIL TO DO THE SOMETHING THAT I CAN DO.

[Helen Keller]

Just like Helen Keller, we want to take what talents we have and do all that we can do, every day.

Helen Keller didn't zero in on her weaknesses; she zeroed in on her strengths.

HAVE COURAGE FOR THE GREAT SORROWS IN LIFE, AND PATIENCE FOR THE SMALL ONES.

[Victor Hugo]

Victor Hugo also said that when you have laboriously accomplished your daily tasks, go to sleep in peace, God is awake.

Do your best every day; leave the results up to God.

YESTERDAY'S A CANCELLED CHECK;
TOMORROW'S A PROMISSORY NOTE.
TODAY'S THE ONLY CASH YOU HAVE;
SPEND IT WISELY.

The Bible teaches us to forget those things that are behind and concentrate on those that are before us.

How you spend your time is more important than how you spend your money. Money mistakes can be corrected, but time lives on forever.

Manage your time – you can't store it – you can't buy it – you can't borrow it. You have to use it, second by second, minute by minute, hour by hour, day by day.

THE MORE I WANT TO GET SOMETHING DONE, THE LESS I CALL IT WORK.

[Richard Bach]

Work without a vision, without a purpose, is a task.

Vision without the work is a dream.

Be determined to accomplish good things every day, and you will not call it work.

THE MIDDLE OF EVERY SUCCESSFUL PROJECT LOOKS LIKE A DISASTER.

[Rosabeth Moss Cantor]

In the middle of a project, don't step back and take a look at where you are. Keep your eye on where you're going. Keep on keeping on.

YOU MAY BE DISAPPOINTED IF YOU FAIL, BUT YOU'RE DOOMED IF YOU DON'T TRY.

[Beverly Sills]

The person who's doing nothing never fails, they only fail to have an impact. Failure is never fatal, it's never final. It's a stepping stone to success.

DOING NOTHING FOR THE FEAR OF MAKING A MISTAKE IS THE BIGGEST MISTAKE OF ALL.

[Coach John Wooden]

In baseball, Ty Cobb stole a lot of bases. He was also thrown out often.

Mickey Mantle hit a lot of home runs. He also struck out many times.

Ty Cobb kept on stealing bases; Mickey Mantle kept on swinging.

GOD MUST HAVE LOVED ORDINARY
PEOPLE; HE MADE SO MANY OF THEM.

[Abraham Lincoln]

Olympic Champion Bob Richards always said, "Every day in
this world, ordinary people are doing extraordinary things in
every field of endeavor."

UNLESS YOU ARE WILLING TO DRENCH
YOURSELF IN YOUR WORK BEYOND THE
CAPACITY OF THE AVERAGE PERSON,
YOU'RE JUST NOT CUT OUT FOR
POSITIONS AT THE TOP.

[J. C. Penney]

Get all caught up in your work and it will cease to be work.

When you are getting the job done, accomplishing your goals,
you will soon find yourself at the top, more than likely with a
crowd following.

136

SUCCESS IS MEASURED NOT SO MUCH BY
THE POSITION THAT ONE HAS REACHED
IN LIFE AS BY THE OBSTACLES THAT
HE HAS OVERCOME WHILE TRYING TO
SUCCEED.

[Booker T. Washington]

The bigger the obstacle, the bigger the success. The tougher
the assignment, the bigger the reward.

Tough competitors make us tougher.

THE SECRET OF SUCCESS IS CONSISTENCY OF PURPOSE.

[Benjamin Disraeli]

Calvin Coolidge said nothing in the world will take the place of persistence.

Talent will not; the world is full of unsuccessful people with talent.

Genius will not; unrewarded genius is almost a Proverb.

Education alone will not; the world is full of educated derelicts.

Consistency of purpose is the secret of success.

SOMETIMES OUR BEST IS SIMPLY NOT ENOUGH. WE HAVE TO DO WHAT IS REQUIRED.

[*Sir Winston Churchill*]

Many times I have said to my associates, "You have to do what you have to do to get the job done. Sometimes you have to be better than your best."

139

THAT MAN IS A SUCCESS WHO HAS
LAUGHED OFTEN AND LOVED MUCH, WHO
HAS FILLED HIS NICHE AND LOVED HIS
TASK, WHO LEAVES THE WORLD BETTER
THAN HE FOUND IT, WHO LOOKED FOR
THE BEST IN OTHERS AND GAVE THE
BEST OF HIMSELF.

[Robert Louis Stevenson]

Laugh often and love much. Love your task, your calling.
Work hard at making this world a better place.

Always look for the best in others and give the best of yourself.

DREAM THE BIG DREAM. THERE'S NOTHING IN SMALL DREAMS TO STIR THE BLOOD.

[Walt Disney]

President Theodore Roosevelt taught that it's far better to dare mighty things, to win glorious triumphs, even though checkered by failure, than to pick ranks with those poor spirits who neither enjoy much nor suffer much because they live in the gray twilight that knows not victory nor defeat.

IF I MISS ONE DAY'S PRACTICE, I NOTICE IT. WHEN I MISS TWO DAYS, THE CRITICS NOTICE IT. WHEN I MISS THREE DAYS, THE AUDIENCE NOTICES IT.

[Ignacy Paderewski, Polish Concert Pianist]

All of us need to be reminded to practice more. All of us need to constantly polish our skills in every area of life.

Great performers know they can't miss one day of practice. They know that practice is what keeps them performing at a high level. You may not be a professional athlete or concert pianist, but you still need to rehearse and practice every day.

IT IS THROUGH THEIR WORK THAT MOST
INDIVIDUALS WRITE THE STORY OF
THEIR LIVES – YOU ARE FREE TO BE THE
HERO OR THE VILLAIN.

Sustained success is grounded in character.

Character produces respect.

Respect builds trust.

Trust motivates others to do what we advise them to do.

PEOPLE ARE RICH OR POOR ACCORDING TO WHAT THEY ARE, NOT ACCORDING TO WHAT THEY HAVE.

[Henry Ward Beecher]

What you do is far more important than what you accumulate.

Accumulate good memories. Build strong relationships with your friends. Stimulate your mind with good knowledge.

GIVE, AND IT SHALL BE GIVEN UNTO YOU;
GOOD MEASURE, PRESSED DOWN, AND
SHAKEN TOGETHER, AND RUNNING OVER,
SHALL MEN GIVE INTO YOUR BOSOM.

[Jesus - Luke 6:38 - KJV]

It is more blessed to give than to receive. We want to give of
our money, of our time, of our talent.

Measure a person by what they give in life, not by what they
get in life!

TWENTY PERCENT OF THE POPULATION
OWN EIGHTY PERCENT OF THE PROPERTY
IN ITALY.

[1906 observation by Vilfredo Pareto - The Pareto Principle]

What you do is far more important than what you accumulate.

Accumulate good memories. Build strong relationships with
your friends. Stimulate your mind with good knowledge.

LOYALTY IS SOMETHING YOU GIVE REGARDLESS OF WHAT YOU GET BACK.

[Charlie Tremendous Jones]

In giving loyalty, you are getting more loyalty; and out of loyalty flows other great qualities.

Charlie Jones was a good friend of mine. I loved his enthusiasm. I also loved his loyalty. He was a very loyal friend. Charlie was loyal to his family, his business, and his faith.

KEEP DEVELOPING THE POWER OF PERSEVERANCE IN YOUR LIFE.

[Jack and Garry Kinder]

Consider the perseverance of Abraham Lincoln. At age:

- 22, failed in business.
- 23, ran for legislature and was defeated.
- 24, failed in business.
- 25, finally was elected to the legislature.
- 29, defeated for speaker of the house.
- 34, defeated for congress.
- 39, lost another bid for congress.
- 46, defeated for the senate.
- 47, defeated for Vice President.
- 49, defeated for the senate.
- 51, Abraham Lincoln was elected President of the United States.

WHENEVER ANYTHING IS BEING
ACCOMPLISHED, IT IS BEING DONE,
I HAVE LEARNED, BY A MONOMANIAC
WITH A MISSION.

[Peter Drucker]

Peter Drucker has always been an inspiration to me. He lived
a full life. He was always inspiring others to be at their best.

This vitamin was one of his greatest statements. If you check
the lives of successful people you will find that they were
always passionate about their mission in life.

TO BRING OUT THE BEST IN OTHERS, GIVE THE BEST OF YOURSELF.

[Harvey S. Firestone]

Whether you are a parent, teacher or a business leader, you are always trying to get the best out of others.

Harvey S. Firestone taught me that in order to bring out the best in others you must always give the best of yourself.

I have found that when I give the best of myself and believe the best about others, everybody is a winner.

I DON'T THINK ANYTHING IS UNREALISTIC IF YOU BELIEVE YOU CAN DO IT.

[Mike Ditka]

Mike Ditka is a very good friend of mine. I have enjoyed playing golf with him, listening to him and visiting with him.

One thing I always noticed about Mike — he always looked for the best in others and gave the best of himself.

I have heard him say many times, "Nothing is unrealistic, if you believe you can do it."

ACE IS THE ANSWER.

[Ken Miller]

Ken Miller is a good friend of mine and he taught me to follow this formula:

A – Maintain a good **A**ttitude.
C – Develop **C**haracter in everything you do.
E - Maintain **E**nthusiasm every day.

ACE – one of the greatest words in the English language. In cards, it's the best card you can hold. In tennis, it's the best serve you can deliver. In golf, it's a hole in one.

LIFE IS WHAT WE MAKE IT; IT ALWAYS HAS BEEN AND ALWAYS WILL BE.

[Grandma Moses]

It was Elizabeth Dole who said, "When you are in your 90s and looking back, it's not going to be how much money you made, or how many awards you won, it's really what you stand for. Did you make a positive difference for people?"

I SKATE TO WHERE THE PUCK IS GOING
TO BE, NOT WHERE IT HAS BEEN. THIS IS
AWARENESS.

[Wayne Gretsky]

You need to be aware of everything that's going on around you.

Listen—really listen. Watch body language. Be aware of
what's happening in your business, in your industry, and in
your personal life.

Develop awareness.

IF GOD HAD WANTED US TO TALK MORE THAN LISTEN, HE WOULD HAVE GIVEN US TWO MOUTHS RATHER THAN TWO EARS.

[Ken Blanchard - We Are the Beloved]

There was an old owl who lived in an oak; the more he heard, the less he spoke. The less he spoke, the more he heard. O, if men were like that wise old bird.

When you ask people about the best leader or friend they ever had, one quality is always mentioned – they are good listeners. They have learned to "sort by others." When people say, "It's a beautiful day," they respond by keeping the focus on the speaker. For example, "Sounds like you're pretty happy today." Poor listeners "sort by self." If you express a concern you have, they will express a concern they have.

Test the power of listening for yourself by taking time to listen and focus on others.

[Excerpt from The Heart of a Leader, Ken Blanchard]

PRE-CONCEIVED NOTIONS ARE THE LOCKS ON THE DOOR TO WISDOM.

[Merry Brown]

Ask questions. Know what the situation is before making decisions.

Don't go into business meetings or interviews with pre-conceived notions. Get the facts, make sure they are accurate, and then make the decision.

EACH OF US WILL ONE DAY BE JUDGED
BY OUR STANDARD OF LIFE, NOT BY OUR
STANDARD OF LIVING; BY OUR MEASURE
OF GIVING, NOT BY OUR MEASURE OF
WEALTH; BY OUR SIMPLE GOODNESS,
NOT BY OUR SEEMING GREATNESS.

[William Arthur Ward]

A great author once said, "When the one great scorer comes
to write about your name, he'll not write that you won or lost,
but how you played the game."

What's your standard of life?

What's your measure of giving?

Are you striving to show kindness and goodness every day?

KNOW WHAT YOU BELIEVE. STAND UP FOR WHAT YOU BELIEVE.

Your weak points are revealed by what you fall for; your strong points are shown by what you stand for.

GENIUS IS 1% INSPIRATION AND 99% PERSPIRATION.

[Thomas Edison]

Thomas Edison had a great mind, but he believed in hard work. Hard work will not make you successful, but you can't be successful without working hard.

OBSTACLES ARE THOSE THINGS YOU SEE WHEN YOU TAKE YOUR EYES OFF THE GOAL.

[Hannah More]

Great golfers keep their eye on the green, not on the sand trap. They keep their eye on where the ball needs to go, not on the water hazard.

The same is true in life. Keep your eye on your goal.

SUCCESS IS A PROCESS, NOT AN EVENT.

Success is not a trophy that you put in the trophy case and say I'm successful. It is not something you achieve once. Lasting success is pursued and cultivated on a daily basis.

161

IF THOU FAINT IN THE DAY OF ADVERSITY, THY STRENGTH IS SMALL.

[Proverbs 24:10 - KJV]

We are not made in a crisis, we are revealed in a crisis.

With every adversity there is sown the seed of an equivalent success.

Keep on keeping on!

Do the right things - in the right way – every day!

162

ANYTHING WORTH DOING IS WORTH
DOING WELL.

Jan Loy, long-time friend and life coach, writes the following
on her blog: In life and in your business, anything worth doing
deserves some thought and planning. It also means that it's
wise to use a plan that's already been proven.

FOR EVERY WRONG, THERE IS A RIGHT.

A young teenager competing for Miss Texas took this
philosophy on as her platform.

All of us need to take it on as our personal theme. Let's focus
on what's right!

CHANCE FAVORS THOSE IN MOTION.

[James H. Austin]

Keep moving. Stay in motion.

In basketball, the team that stays in motion has a better chance of winning - even if they make mistakes.

Conrad Hilton said, "Success seems to be connected with action. Successful people keep moving. They make mistakes, but they don't quit."

Get up and get moving!

WHEN WE'VE DONE OUR BEST, WE
SHOULD WAIT FOR THE RESULTS IN
PEACE.

[John Lubbock]

Be at your best, every day! Do everything to the best of your
ability and leave the results in the hands of God.

LIFE IS NOT ABOUT WAITING FOR THE STORMS TO PASS . . . IT'S ABOUT LEARNING HOW TO DANCE IN THE RAIN.

There are good days and bad days. There's sunshine and rain.

Anybody can be successful when everything is going just right. Great people succeed, even when it rains. Keep on keeping on when it rains.

FAITH IS TAKING THE FIRST STEP, EVEN WHEN YOU DON'T SEE A STAIRCASE.

[Martin Luther King, Jr.]

Always be willing to take that first step. Somebody will be there to help you take the second step.

Many times you can't see the light at the end of the tunnel. Keep going anyway and soon the light will appear.

IT'S OUR ATTITUDE IN LIFE THAT
DETERMINES LIFE'S ATTITUDE TOWARD
US.

[Earl Nightingale]

Our attitude is more important than our talent. Our attitude
determines our altitude.

YOU CAN HAVE ANYTHING YOU WANT IN
LIFE IF YOU JUST HELP ENOUGH OTHER
PEOPLE GET WHAT THEY WANT.

[Zig Ziglar]

Zig Ziglar has spent his life in the business of helping others
get what they want in life. In helping others, we get what we
want in life.

170

WE NEED TO DEVELOP CHARACTER
QUALITIES LIKE INTEGRITY,
TRUSTWORTHINESS, RESPECTABILITY,
UNSELFISHNESS, SELF DISCIPLINE, SELF
CONTROL AND COURAGE.

Virtues like these reflect the image of God and man. Many
times it's called godly character.

Determine to continually develop these character qualities.
Charlie Jones taught me that if you don't use them, you lose
them.

TO BE WHAT WE ARE, AND BECOME WHAT WE ARE CAPABLE OF BECOMING IS THE ONLY END IN LIFE.

[Robert Louis Stevenson]

Keep looking everyday at becoming the person you were created to be. Never stop growing. Strive to be better and better.

172

THE SECRET OF MY SUCCESS: I NEVER GAVE NOR TOOK AN EXCUSE.

[Florence Nightingale]

Allowing oneself to make excuses opens the door in your mind to failure. It's more productive to take responsibility for your choices.

When someone offers an excuse, help them turn that excuse into a stepping stone toward success by taking responsibility for their results.

173

PROGRESS ALWAYS INVOLVES RISK. YOU
CANNOT STEAL SECOND BASE AND KEEP
YOUR FOOT ON FIRST.

[Frederick B. Wilcox]

Every day we wake up, there is risk involved. Every step we
take, there's a risk.

To move ahead, to make progress, there's always risk
involved. Anytime you set a goal and make it public, there's a
risk.

Risk anyway!

ALWAYS PLAY TO WIN.

Nobody remembers who came in second. In 1 Corinthians
we read, "Do you not know that in a race all the runners run,
but only one gets the prize? Run in such a way as to get the
prize."

Always strive to win in everything you do.

IT AIN'T OVER 'TIL IT'S OVER.

[Yogi Berra]

In athletics and in life, you keep playing right to the end.

Always be at your best, even when it looks like there's no hope.

176

WINNERS ARE NOT THOSE WHO NEVER FAIL, BUT THOSE WHO NEVER QUIT.

One time a great baseball player returned home from the minor leagues and told his mother that he was quitting baseball. His mother said, "You do not need to come back here, we don't have any quitters in this house."

Eddie Stanky went back, stuck with the program and became one of the greatest infielders in the history of the major leagues.

BE MORE CONCERNED WITH YOUR CHARACTER THAN YOUR REPUTATION.

Your character is what you really are, while your reputation is merely what others think you are.

It has been said that character is what a man does in the dark. It's what you do when nobody is looking.

THERE IS NO RIGHT WAY TO DO THE WRONG THING.

There are many ways to do the right thing. There's no right way to do the wrong thing.

You can rationalize, you can justify all you want to, but in the end, doing the wrong thing is still doing the wrong thing.

DO THE MATH. COUNT YOUR BLESSINGS.

Remember the words from an old hymn, "Count your blessings, name them one by one."

You need to do that regularly. All of us have much for which to be thankful.

180

SILENCE IS OFTEN MISINTERPRETED, BUT NEVER MISQUOTED.

Many times, the best thing we can do is be quiet. There's a time to speak and there is also a time to remain silent. Many times people just want us to listen, not talk.

THE MOST IMPORTANT THINGS IN YOUR HOME ARE THE PEOPLE.

Many people acquire assets. They buy grown-up toys.

The most important thing in any home, or any business, is the people. Be sure you are building relationships for these are things that last.

A GRUDGE IS A HEAVY THING TO CARRY.

You should never carry a grudge because you'll become like the person you are carrying the grudge against.

Try your best to forgive and forget and move on.

SUCCESS DOESN'T COME TO YOU, YOU GO TO IT.

[Marva Collins]

Success is not a matter of chance; success is a matter of choice. It is in your hands.

Choose success!

3rd
QUARTER

The first 19 vitamins of the 3rd quarter I learned from Dale Carnegie.

As a young man, I took the Dale Carnegie course and it had a great impact on my life. I read for the first time the book entitled, How to Win Friends and Influence People.

The book couldn't have been written at a better time following the Stock Market crash in 1929. It went to the top of the bestseller list and stayed there for ten years.

AVOID ARGUMENTS.

[Dale Carnegie - Influence and Leadership]

Arguments rarely bring about a resolution, whether it's
between parents and children, husband and wife, teacher and
student, or employer and employee. Be determined to stay
away from this exercise that saps you of your strength. It will
lead you nowhere.

DON'T POINT OUT WHEN PEOPLE ARE WRONG. RESPECT DIFFERING VIEWPOINTS.

[Dale Carnegie - Influence and Leadership]

Try to always tell people what to do right, not what they are doing wrong. Most people know when they are doing something wrong. They need a coach that can help them do it right.

WHEN YOU ARE WRONG, ADMIT IT EMPHATICALLY AND MOVE ON.

[Dale Carnegie - Influence and Leadership]

We all make mistakes. When you do, admit it and move on. It's best to say, "I just plain made a mistake. I'm sorry, let's move forward."

YOU WILL GET MORE IN BUSINESS WITH
HONEY THAN VINEGAR. BE FRIENDLY AND
GENTLE.

[Dale Carnegie - Influence and Leadership]

Be nice to everybody you meet. Be friendly, be gentle, and be
optimistic. Be like the fire in the fireplace that attracts people
because it's warm, gentle, inviting.

188

WHEN YOU BEGIN A CONVERSATION WITH
SOMEONE – EVEN IF IT'S AN OPPONENT
– FOCUS ON THINGS UPON WHICH YOU
AGREE.

[Dale Carnegie - Influence and Leadership]

Always try and find common ground. Find out what people's
strengths are and then build on them. Find out what they are
interested in, then talk about it.

LET THE OTHER PERSON TALK MORE THAN YOU DO. LISTEN FULLY.

[Dale Carnegie - Influence and Leadership]

Ask questions and listen. Listen fully. Listen actively. Focus on their needs, their desires, and their ambitions.

190

LEAD PEOPLE TO THE CONCLUSION YOU WANT BY MAKING SUGGESTIONS. ULTIMATELY LET A PERSON FEEL THE IDEA WAS HIS OR HERS.

[Dale Carnegie - Influence and Leadership]

One of our ten cardinal rules of selling is to always make it the prospect's idea. Find out what people want in life, then help them get it. Find out where they want to go and show them how they can get there.

TRY HONESTLY TO SEE THINGS FROM THE OTHER PERSON'S VIEWPOINT.

[Dale Carnegie - Influence and Leadership]

Questions, such as the following, will help you implement this mental vitamin in your daily life. What do you think? What is your opinion? What's your viewpoint on this subject? These are the kinds of questions that help you win friends and influence people.

BELIEVE PEOPLE ARE INHERENTLY GOOD AND HONEST.

[Dale Carnegie - Influence and Leadership]

"We know from a biblical standpoint that people are inherently evil. In your personal relationships, however, you want to treat people as if they are honest. You want to expect them to do the right thing. Always err on the side of being optimistic about how people are going to perform."

USE SHOWMANSHIP OR DRAMATIC TECHNIQUES TO SELL YOUR PRODUCT.

[Dale Carnegie - Influence and Leadership]

You always want to get your point across with stories, with concepts, with metaphors. Be genuine, sincere, colorful, enthusiastic, and optimistic.

194

CREATE COMPETITION IN THE SPIRIT OF A DESIRE TO EXCEL TO GET THE BEST OUT OF YOUR PEOPLE.

[Dale Carnegie - Influence and Leadership]

Competition brings out the best in people. Competition is healthy. Remember, however, when the competition is over you should never compare to other people; you should always compare to how you should have performed according to your abilities.

WHEN POINTING OUT SOMEONE'S MISTAKES TALK ABOUT THEM INDIRECTLY.

[Dale Carnegie - Influence and Leadership]

In helping people with their mistakes you want to coach confidence. Keep watching until they do something right and then praise them. Emphasize the right way to do things rather than point out where people have done it wrong.

TALK ABOUT YOUR OWN FALLIBILITY BEFORE POINTING OUT SOMEONE ELSE'S.

[Dale Carnegie - Influence and Leadership]

It's always good to say to people, "We all make mistakes. I personally have made more than my share. Remember we want to move forward and learn from our mistakes."

USE QUESTIONS TO LEAD PEOPLE INSTEAD OF GIVING DIRECT ORDERS.

[Dale Carnegie - Influence and Leadership]

Instead of saying, you need to do it this way, ask the question, how do you think we ought to do it? What's your opinion? What do you think? These are great questions, whether it's in family life or the business world.

LET OTHER PEOPLE MAINTAIN THEIR PRIDE.

[Dale Carnegie - Influence and Leadership]

You want people to take pride in their performance. You want them to have pride in the outfit. You want them to have confidence in the leadership. Help people be proud of their performance. Once again, you must be genuine.

LAVISH PRAISE ANYTIME YOU SEE AN IMPROVEMENT.

[Dale Carnegie - Influence and Leadership]

Praise in public, praise in private; criticize not at all.

Many times, praising people in a private place is more effective than public praise. Use both lavishly. You'll see improvement in your family, friends and your associates.

SEE THE BEST IN PEOPLE AND THEN THEY WILL RISE TO YOUR EXPECTATION.

[Dale Carnegie - Influence and Leadership]

Always look for the best in people. Expect the best, not perfection. Always bring out the best in others by giving the best of yourself.

201

BE SUPPORTIVE AND MAKE MISTAKES SEEM EASY TO CORRECT.

[Dale Carnegie - Influence and Leadership]

Be supportive. Build people up. Help people see that with minor adjustments they can overcome their mistakes.

WHEN YOU WANT PEOPLE TO DO THINGS THE WAY YOU SUGGEST, POINT OUT THE BENEFITS.

[Dale Carnegie - Influence and Leadership]

Always help people see what the added value is for them by doing the right things in the right way. Help people to keep their eye on the goal, the benefits, and the rewards of doing the right things in the right way.

SUCCESS IS A JOURNEY, NOT A DESTINATION.

The doing is usually more important than the outcome.

If you stop and think about it, every time you have been successful at anything, the path that took you there is what you value most – not the prize.

And that is enough to keep us moving from success to success.

OUR GREATEST FAILURES CAN PRODUCE OUR GREATEST SUCCESSES.

Abraham Lincoln lost the first seven elections he entered.

Helen Keller was born deaf and blind and said, "I thank God for my handicaps."

STRENGTH DOES NOT COME FROM
PHYSICAL CAPACITY; IT COMES FROM AN
INDOMITABLE WILL.

[Mahatma Ghandi]

Many people are physically strong and mentally weak.

Some people are physically strong, mentally strong, but don't
have the will to continue on, no matter what.

Arthur Helps, English historian and novelist, said, "Strength is
born in the deep silence of long-suffering hearts, not amid joy."

There are many things in life that we enjoy. We need to enjoy
our children and our grandchildren. There are many things
in life to enjoy, but our strengths will be developed during
hardship and long-suffering.

YOUR STRUGGLES DEVELOP YOUR STRENGTHS.

The California Redwoods tower above all other trees at 375 feet. These trees date back almost 2000 years.

The scientific name, Sequoia Sempervirens, means "ever living." These older trees have gained strength because they have survived fires, floods and windstorms.

CHOOSE TO SERVE, RATHER THAN BE SERVED.

In Matthew 20:25-28 we read, "But Jesus called them unto him, and said, Ye know that the princes of the Gentiles exercise dominion over them, and they that are great exercise authority upon them. But it shall not be so among you: but whosoever will be great among you, let him be your minister; And whosoever will be chief among you, let him be your servant: Even as the Son of man came not to be ministered unto, but to minister, and to give his life a ransom for many."

LEADERSHIP BEGINS WITH A CLEAR VISION.

There are two parts of leadership; doing the right thing and doing things right.

Always do the right thing, the right way, every day.

THE ENGINE THAT DRIVES ENTERPRISE IS NOT THRIFT, BUT PROFIT.

[John Maynard Keynes]

Many people run a business and try to save on expenses. Others run a business and emphasize gross revenues.

The key is profit. In any enterprise, business or personal, your profit is not what you take in; your true profit is what you save and what you are able to give.

This is true in your business life; this is true in your personal life.

THE ULTIMATE MASTER KEY TO LIFE,
HAPPINESS, AND SUCCESS IS TO FOCUS
ON FIRST THINGS FIRST.

[Howard Wight]

Focus on first things first -- one thing at a time, one step at
a time, one day at a time. Simplify your life. Eliminate the
useless, the unnecessary, and the unimportant.

THE HEART OF THE PRUDENT GETTETH KNOWLEDGE, AND THE EAR OF THE WISE SEEKETH KNOWLEDGE.

[Proverbs 18:15 - KJV]

The intelligent man is always open to new ideas. In fact, he looks for them. High achievers are always looking for the better way.

Keep repeating to yourself: "Every day, in every way, I'm getting better and better."

DON'T WORK HARDER – WORK SMARTER.

This saying is common sense but not common practice. Most people still think there is a direct relationship between the amount of work they do and success – the more time you put in, the more successful you will be.

There is no connection between the number of hours worked and success.

While successful people do work hard, they think before they act. They are proactive, not just reactive. If you don't take time out to think, strategize and prioritize, you will work a whole lot harder, without enjoying the benefits of a job smartly done.

Excerpt from The Heart of a Leader, Ken Blanchard

213

IN ANY ORGANIZATION, ANY EMPLOYEE
TENDS TO RISE TO HIS LEVEL OF
INCOMPETENCE.

[Dr. Laurence J. Peter - Author, The Peter Principle]

In a hierarchical organization, members are promoted so long
as they work competently. Sooner or later they are promoted
to a position at which they are no longer competent (their
"level of incompetence"), and there they remain.

In leadership, we want to make sure that we have the right
people in the right jobs. We also want to make sure that we
don't promote people above their level of competence.

Know your limits, know what you can do and know what you
can't do. It's always best to perform at a level where you are
most competent.

WHEN PEOPLE GO TO WORK, THEY SHOULDN'T HAVE TO LEAVE THEIR HEARTS AT HOME.

[Betty Bender]

Whatever it is you are going to do, do it with your whole heart.

If you're running your household, run it with your whole heart – every dish that's washed, every load of laundry, every child tucked into bed – do it with your whole heart.

If you're running a business, make every decision with your whole heart.

NO MAN WILL MAKE A GREAT LEADER
WHO WANTS TO DO IT ALL HIMSELF, OR
TO GET ALL THE CREDIT FOR IT.

[Andrew Carnegie]

All great leaders learn to delegate. They also learn not to
gather the credit.

Be sure to give others all the credit they are due.

A BOSS SAYS, "GO"; A LEADER SAYS, "LET'S GO."

[E. M. Kelly]

Which are you – Leader or Boss?

Leader	Boss
Builds on strengths	Points out weakness
Coaches confidence	Drives people
Depends on good will	Depends on authority
Inspires enthusiasm	Inspires fear
Says "We"	Says "I"

DEPEND ON INFLUENCE, NOT AUTHORITY.

Ken Blanchard has always said the key to success in
leadership today is influence, not authority.

It's not the power of the job title; it's the power of influence the
leader brings to the job every day.

218

LEADERSHIP HAS ITS REWARDS AND
CHALLENGES, BUT THERE IS ANOTHER
ASPECT TO CONSIDER AND THAT IS, THE
DEBT OF LEADERSHIP.

[Jan Loy - Learning Leadership]

The "Debt of Leadership" – the things you "owe" to those you influence – must be paid each day. As it is paid, you will find that what you have invested will begin to multiply and return to you. Your diligence in leadership will not only "pay off" for you but for those you influence as well.

The next five vitamins will focus on different aspects of this "Debt of Leadership."

I OWE EXCELLENCE.

[Jan Loy - Learning Leadership]

You should be the very best you can be as a person and as a
leader. This means you must continue to grow.

I OWE DECISIVENESS.

[Jan Loy - Learning Leadership]

You must be able to make good, informed decisions even in difficult circumstances. This means you must gather information and learn to apply wisdom.

I OWE WHAT I KNOW.

[Jan Loy - Learning Leadership]

You must be willing to share insights and constructive criticism
in a helpful way. This means you must learn from your
victories as well as your mistakes.

I OWE RIGHT RELATIONSHIPS.

[Jan Loy - Learning Leadership]

As much as possible, you should be at peace with others.
This means you must practice forgiveness and reconciliation.
You must take time to notice the positive in others.
This means you will give credit to others for their
accomplishments.

I OWE GRATITUDE.

[Jan Loy - Learning Leadership]

You must practice a thankful attitude in the situations you face. This means you will express gratitude for the blessings, the opportunities, the resources and the people who walk alongside you.

224

HELP OTHER PEOPLE AND YOUR FAMILY MEMBERS BELIEVE IN THEMSELVES.

Sam Walton said, "Outstanding leaders go out of their way to boost the self-esteem of their personnel. If people believe in themselves, it's amazing what they can accomplish."

225

IN BUSINESS AND IN FAMILY LIFE, DON'T
OVER MANAGE AND UNDER LEAD.

Failing organizations and family situations are usually over
managed and under led.

Remember, most people don't want to be managed, but they
love to be led. You lead people, you manage things.

226

BUILD PEOPLE. FAIL YOUR FAILURES FAST.

Jack Welch taught me to carry a bottle of water in one hand
and fertilizer in the other. Put water on the employees who
are seeds and watch their gardens grow. You'll get some
weeds. Cut out the weeds and eventually reap a gorgeous
garden.

SURROUND YOURSELF WITH THE BEST
PEOPLE YOU CAN FIND, DELEGATE
AUTHORITY AND DON'T INTERFERE.

[Ronald Reagan]

President Ronald Reagan believed in surrounding himself with
good people. He would then delegate almost everything to
them. He would rarely, if ever, interfere. What an example for
the rest of us to follow!

MAKE EVERY DECISION AS IF YOU OWN THE WHOLE COMPANY.

[Robert Townsend]

I have an essay titled, "Act as Though You Own the Place."
Whether you're the owner, the leader or the employee, always
act as if you own the place. This will help you be satisfied with
your work. It will also keep you in a position to be promoted to
the next level.

NEVER CONFUSE ACTIVITY WITH ACHIEVEMENT.

Activity is important, but results are the final judge.

Words are words; explanations are explanations; excuses are excuses; only results are reality.

TELL ME AND I'LL FORGET, SHOW ME AND
I MAY REMEMBER, INVOLVE ME AND I'LL
UNDERSTAND.

[Chinese Proverb]

It's important to inform and instruct people, but it's far more
important to involve people in what you are trying to get
accomplished. You'll get the job done in a far more effective
and efficient manner.

231

LEARN TO GET ALONG WITH THE TOP PERFORMERS.

One time Joe McCarthy was asked, "How do you get along with a sensitive man like Ted Williams?" His answer was, "I get along with any human being who has a batting average over 400."

YOUR DAILY MENTAL VITAMIN /235

232

KNOW YOUR CUSTOMER; TAKE CARE OF YOUR CUSTOMER AND YOUR CUSTOMER WILL TAKE CARE OF YOU.

The great W. Edwards Deming always said, "Profit in business comes from retaining customers – customers who boast about your products or service. They will always bring their friends with them."

Take care of your customers.

233

ANYBODY CAN CUT PRICES, BUT IT TAKES
BRAINS TO PRODUCE A BETTER ARTICLE.

[Philip Armour]

People are attracted to quality. They will pay a higher price
if they get better service. Always strive to produce a better
article and better service.

THERE IS NO SECURITY ON THIS EARTH;
THERE IS ONLY OPPORTUNITY.

[Douglas MacArthur]

Security is important, but what's the opportunity? Security
gives you peace of mind, but opportunity gives you
excitement.

Start looking for jobs that give you an opportunity to achieve –
to be at your best and to use your talents.

I DON'T MEASURE A MAN'S SUCCESS BY
HOW HIGH HE CLIMBS, BUT HOW HIGH HE
BOUNCES WHEN HE HITS THE BOTTOM.

[General George S. Patton]

Earl Nightingale always told us that you judge a person on how
they bounce when they hit bottom. Then he added, "Please
note I said when, not if."

236

WHENEVER AN INDIVIDUAL DECIDES THAT SUCCESS HAS BEEN ATTAINED, PROGRESS STOPS.

[Thomas J. Watson, Jr.]

Yesterday is gone, tomorrow is in the future. The only day you have is today.

There is more to be done. There is more for you to do. The world needs people to encourage continual progress – to inspire the desire to build upon one success after the other.

WHOSO LOVETH INSTRUCTION LOVETH
KNOWLEDGE: BUT HE THAT HATETH
REPROOF IS BRUTISH.

[Proverbs 12:1 - KJV]

To learn, you must want to be taught. Be a lifetime student.

Study your business. Study your competition. Study your
results.

Know what you know. Become known for what you know.

THERE IS NOTHING SO USELESS AS
DOING EFFICIENTLY THAT WHICH SHOULD
NOT BE DONE AT ALL.

[Peter Drucker]

Peter Drucker is the management consultant that gave me the
philosophy regarding efficiency versus effectiveness. He said
efficiency is doing things right; effectiveness is doing the right
things right.

Make sure you are always working on the right things.

IT'S WHAT YOU LEARN AFTER YOU KNOW IT ALL THAT COUNTS.

Have you ever noticed that the more you know, the more you need to know? And as you continue to learn, the result is you just keep getting better and better.

Keep learning and growing.

DON'T EVER TALK UNTIL YOU KNOW WHAT YOU ARE TALKING ABOUT.

We all learn more by listening than we do by talking. A wise man said, "Never speak until you have something to say."

CHARACTER IS WHAT A MAN IS IN THE DARK.

The book of James tells us a double-minded man is unstable in all his ways. Another way to express this is that people of character do what's right, even when no one is looking.

NEVER SETTLE FOR ACCEPTABLE.
ALWAYS GO FOR EXCEPTIONAL.

[Og Mandino]

Og Mandino taught me many things. This is one of his greatest thoughts. Everything you do, do it to the best of your ability. Never do anything just to be acceptable. Do everything you do to be exceptional.

EVEN IF YOU ARE ON THE RIGHT TRACK, YOU'LL GET RUN OVER IF YOU JUST SIT THERE.

It's not enough to be on the right track. You must be moving in the right direction and you must be achieving a consistent speed ahead.

244

PEOPLE FORGET HOW FAST YOU DID YOUR JOB, BUT THEY NEVER FORGET HOW WELL YOU DID IT.

Do everything you do with quality. People don't remember the speed, but they'll always remember the quality. Stamp everything you do with excellence.

NEVER! NEVER! NEVER! NEVER! GIVE UP!

[Winston Churchill]

In his later years, Winston Churchill gave a speech at the English prep school he attended as a boy. The headmaster told the boys, "This is an historic moment. Winston Churchill is the greatest speaker of the English language. Write down everything he says. He will make an unforgettable speech."

When Churchill walked out to give his speech, he peered over the top of his glasses and said, "Never! Never! Never! Never! Give up!" With that, he sat down. Many students were disappointed, but the headmaster felt this might have been one of Churchill's greatest speeches. If one quality epitomized Winston Churchill, it was persistence. He never gave up. It was that attitude that inspired England in World War II to continue fighting when others might have surrendered.

Persistence means sticking to your guns, making good on your commitments and making your actions consistent with your words.

Excerpt from The Heart of a Leader, Ken Blanchard

246

IT'S OKAY TO BE CONTENT WITH WHAT YOU HAVE, BUT NEVER BE CONTENT WITH WHAT YOU ARE.

It's far more important to be concerned about what you are than what you have. Keep improving what you are and you will find that what you have is quite enough.

247

TO DO BETTER, YOU MUST FIRST BE BETTER.

The world is full of unsuccessful people with talent. The parable of the talents teaches us to take the talent we have and use it to the best of our abilities.

THE PURPOSE OF LIFE IS A LIFE OF PURPOSE.

[Robert Byrne]

Know your mission. Know your purpose.   Develop a passion for your purpose.

A person going through life with a passion for what they are doing is unstoppable.

IF YOUR PRINCIPLES BECOME DATED, THEY ARE NOT PRINCIPLES.

The Ten Commandments haven't changed in 5000 years. The Sermon on the Mount is still relevant.

We all need unchanging principles and philosophies that guide us, no matter which way the winds are blowing.

IDEAS AND INFORMATION HAVE ZERO VALUE UNTIL THEY ARE IMPLEMENTED.

The payoff always comes in the execution. Execution means to finalize, to put into action. The people that execute are more important to an organization than are the creators.

WE ARE WHAT WE REPEATEDLY DO. EXCELLENCE THEN, IS NOT AN ACT, BUT A HABIT.

.

Don't do things right once in awhile, do them right all the time. We want to build on excellence and we want it to become a habit.

LEARN FROM OTHERS. BELIEVE IN OVERCOMPENSATION. NEVER FOLLOW THE LINE OF LEAST RESISTANCE.

[Coach Frank Leahy - Notre Dame University]

Coach Leahy taught that these attitudes overcome the opposition and bring victory. He preached overcompensation.

Coach Leahy taught that your weakness can become your greatest strength. He also taught that if you are not careful, your strength can become your weakness.

THE POWER OF COMMUNICATION LIES IN ITS SIMPLICITY.

[Dr. Kenneth McFarland]

In anything you do, keep it simple. This is true for public speaking, it's true for selling, and it's true for everything in communication.

Your power in communicating will come from taking the complex and making it simple.

YOU CAN'T LOSE SOMETHING YOU NEVER HAD.

[Fred Holderman]

There will always be competition in sales or any walk of life. Whether it's the business world or your personal life, you are always going to strive to get the business, win the contest.

When it's all over, remember, you can't lose something you never had.

HE THAT TILLETH HIS LAND SHALL
HAVE PLENTY OF BREAD, BUT HE THAT
FOLLOWETH AFTER VAIN PERSONS, SHALL
HAVE POVERTY ENOUGH.

[Proverbs 28:19 - KJV]

There are two great messages here:

- Do your work, it can cure a lot of your ills and you will always have money.
- Keep away from people who are not focused on the right things. If you are going to follow someone, make sure they are going where you want to go and that they are out in front of you.

256

ENTER NOT INTO THE PATH OF THE
WICKED, AND GO NOT IN THE WAY OF
EVIL MEN.

[Proverbs 4:14 - KJV]

Walk with wise people, learn from them.

Run away from those that are evil – those who are always
looking for a shortcut to success.

257

SUCCESSFUL PEOPLE MOVE ON THEIR INITIATIVE, BUT THEY KNOW WHERE THEY ARE GOING BEFORE THEY START.

All successful people have a goal of where they are going. They also have a plan of action as to how to reach their goal.

It's not enough just to set the goal – you have to set the plan of action.

IDEAS AND CONCEPTS CHANGE PEOPLE'S LIVES. IDEAS AND CONCEPTS ARE WHAT HAVE CHANGED CIVILIZATIONS.

There's an old Oriental Proverb that says, "If you would plant for days, plant flowers; if you would plant for years, plant trees; if you plant for eternity, plant ideas."

259

A JOURNEY OF A THOUSAND MILES
BEGINS WITH ONE STEP.

A little job well done is the first step toward a bigger one.

How do you eat an elephant? One bite at a time.

How do you read a book? One page at a time.

Start the journey and everything else will follow.

260

NO PERSON CAN BECOME A PERMANENT SUCCESS WITHOUT TAKING OTHERS ALONG.

Successful people attract others to them. Success is rarely an accident; it is also rarely achieved completely by oneself.

RENDER MORE AND BETTER SERVICE
THAN THAT FOR WHICH YOU ARE
PAID AND, SOONER OR LATER, YOU
WILL RECEIVE COMPOUND INTEREST
ON COMPOUND INTEREST FOR YOUR
INVESTMENT.

[Napoleon Hill]

Do more than you are paid for and eventually you will be paid
a lot more than you are worth. It's called going the extra mile.

Be determined to always do your best for your customers ...
and then some.

Everybody has customers!

262

THE GREATEST OF ALL GIFTS IS THE GIFT OF AN OPPORTUNITY FOR A PERSON TO MAKE GOOD ON THEIR OWN MERITS.

Take advantage of every opportunity that comes your way. That's all we need is opportunity, then our talents, our energy, and our desire will take us to greatness.

BE VERY CAREFUL WHAT YOU SET YOUR
HEART ON, FOR YOU WILL SURELY
ACHIEVE IT.

[French Proverb]

Keep your mind on the things you want and off the things you
don't want. Every day, get up and keep focused on the goal.

264

TO BE ENTHUSIASTIC, YOU MUST FIRST ACT ENTHUSIASTIC.

Be determined to start each day in an enthusiastic manner.

Remember, that feelings always follow actions. So get up and get into action and do it enthusiastically.

CONCENTRATION IS THE SECRET OF
STRENGTH IN POLITICS, IN WAR, IN
TRADE; IN SHORT, IN ALL MANAGEMENT
OF HUMAN AFFAIRS.

[Emerson]

Develop the ability to concentrate, to focus, to pay attention.
In almost any endeavor, this becomes a key attribute. Work at
developing it on a daily basis.

EVERY DEFEAT, EVERY DISAPPOINTMENT,
AND EVERY ADVERSITY CARRIES SEEDS
OF EQUIVALENT BENEFITS.

[W. Clement Stone]

Every disappointment and every setback is a stepping stone.
It depends on whether or not you choose to take the first step
to find the benefit.

A SOUND MIND IN A SOUND BODY IS A
SHORT, BUT FULL DESCRIPTION OF A
HAPPY STATE IN THIS WORLD.

[John Locke]

You want to stay active and fit and mentally alert.

Dr. Ken Cooper, known as the "Father of Aerobics," says we
want more people who are just as energetic at 5 PM as they
are at 8 AM. His book, *Aerobics,* is one that everybody needs
to read.

WHAT YOU GET BY REACHING YOUR
DESTINATION ISN'T NEARLY AS
IMPORTANT AS WHAT YOU BECOME
REACHING THAT DESTINATION.

Many times the journey is far more rewarding than the actual
destination. It's the struggle along the way that pays big
dividends.

YOU CANNOT PLOW A FIELD BY TURNING IT OVER IN YOUR MIND.

Jan Loy tells us to be competitive, to obligate ourselves to doing something specific. She gives us the four "D's" of commitment:

- Desire
- Decision
- Determination
- Discipline

These are more than words; these are things that will help you be committed and stay committed to reaching your goals.

270

LIFE IS LIKE RIDING A BICYCLE;
TO KEEP YOUR BALANCE, YOU MUST
KEEP MOVING.

[Albert Einstein]

Stay on the move. People who get on in this world are the people who take action.

Be sure you are moving in the right direction, but most important of all, keep moving.

YOU HAVE TO HAVE SOMETHING YOU
BELIEVE IN. IT CAN BE SOMEONE YOU
BELIEVE IN. IT HAS TO BE SOMETHING
YOU BELIEVE IN THAT YOU CAN'T BE
TALKED OUT OF BY DOLLARS AND CENTS.

[George Foreman]

Know what you believe about the important things in life. What
is it you believe in so strongly you could never be backed
down, no matter what?

Know what you believe. Practice what you believe. Be
persistent on what you believe.

272

ALWAYS BEAR IN MIND THAT YOUR OWN
RESOLUTION TO SUCCEED IS MORE
IMPORTANT THAN ANY OTHER ONE
THING.

[Abraham Lincoln]

Be determined to succeed. Your own determination and
resolution is the most important thing in success. Be
determined to be what you are created to be.

ONE OF THE GREATEST LESSONS
I HAVE LEARNED IS THAT YOU HAVE TO
DISCIPLINE YOUR LIFE.

[Garry Kinder]

No matter how good you may be, you have to be willing to cut
out of your life those things that keep you from going to the
top.

THE SECRET AND STRENGTH OF MY SUCCESS LIES SOLELY IN TENACITY.

[Louis Pasteur]

Opportunity is missed by most people because it comes disguised as work and dressed in overalls.

275

A GEM CANNOT BE POLISHED WITHOUT
FRICTION, NOR A MAN PERFECTED
WITHOUT TRIALS.

[Chinese Proverb]

Gold is purified by fire and diamonds are made under pressure.

4th
QUARTER

*We start the 4th Quarter with Napoleon Hill's 17 Principles
of Personal Achievement. Napoleon Hill developed these
principles when he wrote his book, Think and Grow Rich.*

This is another book that had a great influence on my life.

Used with permission from The Napoleon Hill Foundation.

LESSON 1:   DEFINITENESS OF PURPOSE

[Napoleon Hill - 17 Principles of Personal Achievement]

Definiteness of purpose is the starting point of all achievement. Without a purpose and a plan, people drift aimlessly through life.

LESSON 2: MASTERMIND ALLIANCE

[Napoleon Hill - 17 Principles of Personal Achievement]

The Mastermind Principle consists of an alliance of two or
more minds working in perfect harmony for the attainment of
a common definite objective. Success does not come without
the cooperation of others.

LESSON 3: APPLIED FAITH

[Napoleon Hill - 17 Principles of Personal Achievement]

Faith is a state of mind through which your aims, desires, plans and purposes may be translated into their physical or financial equivalent.

LESSON 4: GOING THE EXTRA MILE

[Napoleon Hill - 17 Principles of Personal Achievement]

Going the extra mile is the action of rendering more and better service than that for which you are presently paid. When you go the extra mile, the Law of Compensation comes into play.

LESSON 5: PLEASING PERSONALITY

[Napoleon Hill - 17 Principles of Personal Achievement]

Personality is the sum total of one's mental, spiritual and physical traits and habits that distinguish one from all others. It is the factor that determines whether one is liked or disliked by others.

LESSON 6: PERSONAL INITIATIVE

[Napoleon Hill - 17 Principles of Personal Achievement]

Personal initiative is the power that inspires the completion of
that which one begins. It is the power that starts all action.
No person is free until he learns to do his own thinking and
gains the courage to act on his own.

LESSON 7: POSITIVE MENTAL ATTITUDE

[Napoleon Hill - 17 Principles of Personal Achievement]

A positive mental attitude is the right mental attitude in all circumstances. Success attracts more success while failure attracts more failure.

LESSON 8: ENTHUSIASM

[Napoleon Hill - 17 Principles of Personal Achievement]

Enthusiasm is faith in action. It is the intense emotion known as burning desire. It comes from within, although it radiates outwardly in the expression of one's voice and countenance.

LESSON 9: SELF-DISCIPLINE

[Napoleon Hill - 17 Principles of Personal Achievement]

Self-discipline begins with the mastery of thought. If you do
not control your thoughts, you cannot control your needs.
Self-discipline calls for a balancing of the emotions of your
heart with the reasoning faculty of your head.

LESSON 10: ACCURATE THINKING

[Napoleon Hill - 17 Principles of Personal Achievement]

The power of thought is the most dangerous or the most
beneficial power available to man, depending on how it is
used.

LESSON 11: CONTROLLED ATTENTION

[Napoleon Hill - 17 Principles of Personal Achievement]

Controlled attention leads to mastery in any type of human endeavor, because it enables one to focus the powers of his mind upon the attainment of a definite objective and to keep it so directed at will.

LESSON 12: TEAMWORK

[Napoleon Hill - 17 Principles of Personal Achievement]

Teamwork is harmonious cooperation that is willing, voluntary
and free. Whenever the spirit of teamwork is the dominating
influence in business or industry, success is inevitable.
Harmonious cooperation is a priceless asset that you can
acquire in proportion to your giving.

LESSON 13: ADVERSITY AND DEFEAT

[Napoleon Hill - 17 Principles of Personal Achievement]

Individual success usually is in exact proportion of the scope of the defeat the individual has experienced and mastered. Many so-called failures represent only a temporary defeat that may prove to be a blessing in disguise.

LESSON 14: CREATIVE VISION

[Napoleon Hill - 17 Principles of Personal Achievement]

Creative vision is developed by the free and fearless use of one's imagination. It is not a miraculous quality with which one is gifted or is not gifted at birth.

LESSON 15: HEALTH

[Napoleon Hill - 17 Principles of Personal Achievement]

Sound health begins with a sound health consciousness, just as financial success begins with a prosperity consciousness.

LESSON 16: BUDGETING TIME AND MONEY

[Napoleon Hill - 17 Principles of Personal Achievement]

Time and money are precious resources and few people striving for success ever believe they possess either one in excess.

LESSON 17: HABITS

[Napoleon Hill - 17 Principles of Personal Achievement]

Developing and establishing positive habits leads to peace of mind, health and financial security. You are where you are because of your established habits and thoughts and deeds.

HE BECOMETH POOR THAT DEALETH WITH A SLACK HAND: BUT THE HAND OF THE DILIGENT MAKETH RICH.

[Proverbs 10:4 - KJV]

Hard work will not necessarily make you successful. However, you can't be successful without hard work. Lazy men are soon poor; hard workers get rich.

294

ONLY THOSE WHO RISK GOING TOO FAR
WILL EVER KNOW HOW FAR THEY CAN
GO.

To strive for outstanding success is a risk. If you become successful, you have to keep on being successful. You have to keep on reaching out to see how far you can go.

When you've gone as far as you can go, go some more.

THERE'S NO SUCH THING IN ANYONE'S LIFE AS AN UNIMPORTANT DAY.

[Alexander Woollcott]

Make everyday a great day. There are no unimportant days.
Repeat to yourself often that this is the day the Lord hath
made, I will rejoice and be happy in it.

296

A SMILE IS CONTAGIOUS; BE A CARRIER.

It takes fewer muscles to smile than to frown. Smile at people and most of the time they'll smile back.

A great professor in my college days told me to eat a good breakfast and smile at everybody I meet before 10 in the morning, and everything else will take care of itself.

297

IT IS EASIER TO GO DOWN A HILL THAN
UP, BUT THE BEST VIEW IS FROM THE
TOP.

It takes more effort and energy to go up a hill than down a hill.
It is worth the effort, and then some, to see the view from the
top.

298

THE BEST THING TO DO BEHIND A FRIEND'S BACK IS TO PAT IT.

The greatest compliment we can give a person is to say good things about them when they are not there. Naturally, it has to be genuine. A compliment always has a way of getting back to the person you were talking about.

IT IS THE SPIRIT THAT DECIDES WHETHER WE WILL GIVE OUR BEST, FINISH STRONG, OR DO JUST ENOUGH TO GET BY.

Individuals who finish strong have these characteristics. They:

- dream the big dreams
- are practical and realistic
- think greatly of their function
- are appearance conscious
- believe in preparation
- like to be effective
- make responsible commitments
- respond to responsibility
- enjoy improving things
- bounce back

If you are discouraged, remember that your job is to hang in there and finish strong!

YOU ARE THE ONLY PERSON ON THIS EARTH WHO CAN USE YOUR ABILITY.

[Billy Graham]

Mary Crowley, founder of Home Interiors and Gifts, Inc., always told me, "God didn't make any losers. You were born to win."

Everyone has a unique ability. Be sure you are using yours to its fullest extent.

301

PEOPLE PURSUE HAPPINESS AND NEVER
FIND IT. THE WAY TO FIND HAPPINESS
IS TO PURSUE YOUR FAITH, YOUR FAMILY
AND YOUR PROFESSION.

[Bill Bennett]

Happiness is like a butterfly, the more you chase it, the more it
will elude you. But, if you turn your attention to other things, it
comes softly and sits on your shoulder.

This is a Chinese Proverb that Janet Kinder memorized as a
young girl.

302

THE BEST WAY TO FORGET YOUR OWN
PROBLEMS IS TO HELP SOMEONE ELSE
SOLVE THEIRS.

Strive to always get caught up in something bigger than you
are.   If you haven't already discovered it, there are others
all around you who need help – their problems may be worse
than yours. In helping others, we find our troubles either
diminish or are completely eliminated.

303

MEASURE WEALTH NOT BY THE THINGS
YOU HAVE, BUT BY THE THINGS YOU
HAVE FOR WHICH YOU WOULD NOT TAKE
MONEY.

You can buy a doctor's advice, but you can't buy health. You
can buy a counselor's help, but you can't buy peace of mind.
You can buy a house, but you can't buy a home. You can buy
a person's time, but you can't buy their love.

WE NEED TO LEARN TO SET OUR COURSE BY THE STARS, NOT BY THE LIGHT OF EVERY PASSING SHIP.

[Omar Bradley]

Keep your eye on the North Star – your goals. It's okay to compete with other people, but never compare to them. Always compare yourself to what you ought to be. Keep focused on your mission, your goals.

DO NOT FOLLOW WHERE THE PATH MAY
LEAD. GO INSTEAD WHERE THERE IS NO
PATH AND LEAVE A TRAIL.

[Muriel Strode]

Earl Nightingale taught me, never follow the crowd. Down
through history, the crowd has generally been wrong. They
took the wrong path. You're unique, build your own path.

306

ONE OF THE SECRETS OF LIFE IS
TO MAKE STEPPING STONES OUT OF
STUMBLING BLOCKS.

[Jack Penn]

This poem says it all.

Isn't it strange
That princes and kings,
And clowns that caper
In sawdust rings,
And common people
Like you and me
Are builders for eternity?
Each is given a bag of tools,
A shapeless mass,
A book of rules;
And each must make –
Ere life is flown -
A stumbling block
Or a steppingstone.

R.L. Sharpe

307

WHEN I WAS YOUNG I OBSERVED THAT
NINE OUT OF EVERY TEN THINGS I DID
WERE FAILURES, SO I DID TEN TIMES
MORE WORK.

[George Bernard Shaw]

Dr. Norman Vincent Peale reminds me that the only people
who don't make mistakes are in the graveyard. Everybody
makes mistakes. Get up and get going. Remember that failure
is just a temporary setback.

308

THE ONLY PEOPLE YOU SHOULD EVER
WANT TO GET EVEN WITH ARE THOSE
THAT HAVE HELPED YOU.

[John Honeyfeld]

Don't worry about the people that do you wrong. Just keep
going and be about your business. Strive to get even with the
people that have helped you along the way.

309

HE THAT IS SLOW TO ANGER IS BETTER
THAN THE MIGHTY; AND HE THAT RULETH
HIS SPIRIT THAN HE THAT TAKETH A CITY.

[Proverbs 16:32 - KJV]

Many a person has been left behind because they were trying
to control others, instead of controlling their own thinking and
their own actions.

It is better to have self-control than to control an army.

310

WHAT A LOT WE LOST WHEN WE STOPPED WRITING LETTERS. YOU CAN'T REREAD A PHONE CALL.

[Liz Carpenter]

Some of the best things that have happened to me have happened when people sent a personal, handwritten note. The Internet is tremendous; we should use it wisely. But it will never replace the impact of a handwritten note.

THERE'S A TIME TO WEEP AND A TIME TO LAUGH; A TIME TO MOURN AND A TIME TO DANCE.

[Ecclesiastes 3:4 - KJV]

We are also told to weep with those who weep and laugh with those who laugh.

It's important to laugh with your friends and family. It's also important, when grieving, to weep with your friends and family.

312

I HOPE I SHALL ALWAYS POSSESS
FIRMNESS AND VIRTUE ENOUGH TO
MAINTAIN WHAT I CONSIDER THE
MOST ENVIABLE OF ALL TITLES, THE
CHARACTER OF AN HONEST MAN.

[George Washington]

Our first president based everything he did on honesty. No matter what your station is in life, honesty is the best policy. We need to be honest in everything we do and in everything we say.

313

DO YOU WANT TO KNOW WHO YOU ARE? DON'T ASK. ACT! ACTION WILL DELINEATE AND DEFINE YOU.

[Thomas Jefferson]

People wouid rather see a sermon than hear one any day. The Bible teaches us that by their fruits ye shall know them. Your actions define who you are.

314

BELIEVE YOU CAN AND YOU ARE HALF
WAY THERE.

[Theodore Roosevelt]

Set goals that you can believe in 100%. Believe with your
mind and with your heart. Set your goal, believe you can
make it, and you are half way there.

THE ULTIMATE MEASURE OF A MAN IS
NOT WHERE HE STANDS IN MOMENTS
OF COMFORT AND CONVENIENCE,
BUT WHERE HE STANDS AT TIMES OF
CHALLENGE AND CONTROVERSY.

[Martin Luther King, Jr.]

History reveals that both people and nations are at their best
during the toughest of times.

316

THE FLOCK IS NOT THERE FOR THE SAKE
OF THE SHEPHERD; THE SHEPHERD IS
THERE FOR THE SAKE OF THE FLOCK.

[Dr. Ken Blanchard]

The servant leader, the shepherd, helps people improve the
quality of their lives.

TO THINE OWN SELF BE TRUE, AND IT
MUST FOLLOW, AS THE NIGHT THE DAY,
THOU CANST NOT THEN BE FALSE TO ANY
MAN.

[William Shakespeare]

Theodore Roosevelt once said, "I care not what others think
of what I do, but I care very much about what I think of what I
do." That's character!

Constantly, continually strive to improve yourself mentally,
physically, professionally and spiritually.

318

PROVIDE VALUE EVERY DAY AND COMMIT TO IMPROVING YOUR SKILLS EVERY DAY.

[Cal Ripken, Jr.]

Ripkin also taught me to focus on fundamentals. He once said, "Don't get so distracted by record setting or other feats that you neglect to focus on doing your best every day."

ALWAYS STAY BRILLIANT ON THE BASICS.

All the great coaches and all the great business leaders have one thing in common, they are brilliant on the basics. Coaches like Lombardi, Landry and Wooden are examples. They were innovators, yet they never forgot to teach the basics. Read the great books by Lee Iacocca and Jack Welch and you'll find that, like the great coaches, they were brilliant on the basics.

320

YOUR POWER IN SALES AND IN
MANAGEMENT WILL ALWAYS COME FROM
SIMPLICITY.

In 1982, Tom Peters and Robert Waterman wrote a book
entitled, *In Search of Excellence.* It was one of the best
business books in history. In studying the excellent
companies, they found many common denominators. One of
them was: Excellent companies keep it simple in a complex
world.

Great leaders are great simplifiers.

AN OPPORTUNITY IS WORTH TO A PERSON
EXACTLY WHAT THEIR PREPARATION
ENABLES THEM TO MAKE OF IT.

[Dick Vermeil]

Spectacular performance is always preceded by unspectacular
preparation. Preparation never takes place under the bright
lights. It's always done behind the scenes.

There are very few people there to applaud the efforts of
preparation. It's inglorious. It's hard work. It takes discipline,
but it always precedes spectacular performance.

WHATEVER YOU SET OUT TO DO, DO IT WITH ALL YOUR HEART, WITH ALL YOUR MIGHT, WITH ALL YOUR SOUL.

In Ecclesiastes we are taught, "Whatsoever thy hand findeth to do, do it with thy might."

I've always said, "Whatever it is you set out to do, give it everything you've got from the souls of your feet to the top of your head. Lose yourself in getting the job done."

AS YE SOW, SO SHALL YOU REAP, MULTIPLIED.

Most all scientists will agree that one of the greatest laws of nature is as ye sow, so shall you reap, multiplied. You plant corn seeds, you always get corn, multiplied. If you plant apple seeds, you are always going to get apples, multiplied. You plant good thoughts in your mind, you are always going to get a return of good thoughts, multiplied.

324

DON'T WASTE TIME WITH PEOPLE WHO
WASTE YOUR TIME.

There are people who waste your time. These people are not .
going where you want to go. They are going down a different
road, chasing a different goal.

KNOW THE TRUTH AND THE TRUTH SHALL SET YOU FREE.

In Psalm 1:1-2 we read, "Blessed is the man that walketh not in the counsel of the ungodly, nor standeth in the way of sinners, nor sitteth in the seat of the scornful, but his delight is in the law of the Lord and in his law doth he meditate day and night."

326

ACCENTUATE THE POSITIVE AND ELIMINATE THE NEGATIVE.

These words are from a song I used to sing as a kid. But it's also biblical. The Bible tells us whatsoever things are true, honest, just, pure, lovely, things of good report, virtue, if there be any praise, think on these things. This is Philippians 4:8 paraphrased.

327

IT'S BETTER TO LIGHT A CANDLE THAN TO
CURSE THE DARKNESS.

[Chinese Proverb]

Strive to always be part of the solution, not part of the
problem. Instead of complaining and criticizing, be a
compliment carrier.

328

HE IS A WISE MAN WHO DOES NOT GRIEVE FOR THE THINGS WHICH HE HAS NOT, BUT REJOICES FOR THOSE WHICH HE HAS.

[Epictetus]

Keep your eyes on what you have in your possession. Pay attention to, and take care of, what you have. Don't worry about those things that you have not.

329

CAPITALISM WITHOUT FAILURE IS LIKE CHRISTIANITY WITHOUT HELL.

[Warren Buffett]

Life is all about what is right and what is wrong. It's all about winning and losing.

Always do what's right; always do your best. You will win some and you will lose some. Be humble in victory and courageous in defeat.

330

WORDS MATTER; ACTIONS MATTER MORE.

We promise with our words; we inspire with our actions.

In every walk of life we will always be rewarded for our results. Always take the right action and leave the results up to God.

TRUE LOVE WILL FIND AN OUTLET IN SERVICE.

[Billy Graham]

People that succeed are those that learn to serve. Success comes to those who learn how to serve others regularly.

332

YOU MAY FOOL THE WHOLE WORLD DOWN
THE PATHWAY OF LIFE AND GET PATS
ON YOUR BACK AS YOU PASS, BUT YOUR
FINAL REWARD WILL BE HEARTACHES
AND TEARS IF YOU'VE CHEATED THE MAN
IN THE GLASS.

[Dale Wimbrow]

This is the closing verse of a poem given to Norman Vincent
Peale by Lowell Thomas one day after hearing one of Dr.
Peale's sermons. He said, "Frankly, if you had read this
poem, your talk would have been much better." Obviously,
Dr. Peale agreed, because he kept a copy of the poem in his
wallet and referred to it frequently.

While the message is loud and clear, you might ask, "But don't
some people do the wrong thing and then rationalize what
they've done?" Yes, people do that, but if they take a good
hard look at themselves, down deep, they know they have
done wrong.

You can't go against your image of yourself and what you think
is right without feeling bad. It's counter to your purpose – the
picture you have of yourself as an ethical person. A clear purpose
is the foundation upon which sound, ethical behavior is built.

[Excerpt from The Heart of a Leader, Ken Blanchard]

MAKE THE DECISION, THEN, MAKE THE DECISION RIGHT.

[Charlie Jones]

It was H. A. Hopf who said, "Indecision is debilitating. It feeds on itself. It is habit forming. Not only that, it is also contagious; it transmits itself to others."

Make your decisions and then make them right.

334

THROUGH WISDOM IS AN HOUSE
BUILDED; AND BY UNDERSTANDING IT
IS ESTABLISHED: AND BY KNOWLEDGE
SHALL THE CHAMBERS BE FILLED WITH
ALL PRECIOUS AND PLEASANT RICHES.

[Proverbs 24:3-4 - KJV]

Any enterprise is built by wise planning, becomes strong
through common sense and profits by keeping abreast of the
facts.

Develop your plans, install your systems, build your
philosophies, know the facts, good things will happen to you.

LIFE IS SHORT; LIFE IS FRAGILE.

[Dr. W. A. Criswell]

Our life here on this earth is fragile – it is short. Be at your best every day, because you never know.

Just one little dash between two vast eternities – reason enough to be at your best every day.

LOOK FOR EXPERIENCES THAT WILL ALLOW YOU TO GROW.

The finer Japanese restaurants typically put multicolored fish in small ponds. They are like giant goldfish and are beautiful to watch. These colorful fish are referred to as "Japanese carp," but are more properly known as koi.

The interesting thing about the koi is that if you keep it in a small fish bowl, it will grow to be two or three inches long, at most. However, when placed in a huge lake where it can really stretch out its territory, this unique fish will grow to more than three feet in length!

Discipline yourself to think big. Improve your performance. Remove any limitations you have placed on yourself that keep you from growing.

COME UNTO ME, ALL YE THAT LABOUR
AND ARE HEAVY LADEN, AND I WILL GIVE
YOU REST.

[Jesus - Matthew 11:28 - KJV]

Jesus taught us to always turn to him when we become tired,
when our burdens are heavy. He will give us rest and restore
our spirit.

338

KNOW YOUR BUSINESS AND KEEP ON KNOWING YOUR BUSINESS.

If you do not have a research and development department, start one today! Fill it with resources that will inform, instruct, and inspire – tools that will keep you current on your industry and focused on the desired results. It will keep you "above the crowd."

Knowing your business is an investment of time and money that will result in the confidence of your associates and customers.

COURAGE IS MORE EXHILARATING THAN FEAR, AND IN THE LONG RUN IT IS EASIER.

[Eleanor Roosevelt]

Never take counsel of your fears.

Be prepared; be ready and get with the program. Have the courage and the discipline to do what you ought to do.

Do the thing you fear – the fear goes away.

340

WE RUN, NOT BECAUSE WE THINK IT
IS DOING US GOOD, BUT BECAUSE WE
ENJOY IT AND CANNOT HELP OURSELVES.

[Roger Bannister - "How Passion Works"]

You'll live every day in great anticipation when you are driven
by the sheer joy you experience fulfilling your passion.

It cannot be overstated – we must know our purpose and live
with a passion for fulfilling that purpose.

GET AN OUTSIDE PERSPECTIVE.

No individual achieves outstanding success alone. Everyone needs help to learn, grow, and develop skills. You'll be surprised how close that help is, if you attract, nurture and develop a mentor. Here's what you can gain from a mentor:

- Expects the best of you.
- Helps you shortcut time.
- Always available.
- Source of encouragement.
- Serves as a "sounding board."
- Source of knowledge and expertise.
- Holds you to high standards.
- Is concerned about your professional and personal growth.
- Promotes you to others.
- Serves as a valuable role model.

A mentor should be someone traveling the same road you are – and way out in front.

342

SET YOUR EXPECTATIONS HIGH. THEY WILL BE THE LIMIT TO WHICH YOU RISE.

Romana Banuelos had little reason to expect great things for her life. At 18, living in Mexico, her husband deserted her and her two children.

Romana borrowed enough money to buy bus tickets for herself and her children to Los Angeles, CA. She spoke no English and had no skills or training, but she got a job washing dishes in a cafe. After the evening shift was over, she stayed on from midnight to six o'clock in the morning to make tacos. Romana was able to save $400, which she invested in a taco machine. Over the next 20 years, she developed the largest wholesale Mexican food business in the world, Romona's Mexican Food Products.

That is not the end of the story! Because of her accomplishments, Romana Banuelos was frequently cited by the business community. Ultimately, the President of the United States appointed her Secretary of the Treasury, the first Mexican-American, and the sixth woman, to hold the position.

343

THE MOST REWARDING THINGS YOU DO IN LIFE ARE OFTEN THE ONES THAT LOOK LIKE THEY CANNOT BE DONE.

[Arnold Palmer]

Expect to do those things that look like they can't be done. When you set your high expectations, begin to do the little things required to reach those goals. Doing little things well is a necessary step toward doing big things with excellence.

Ask yourself these questions:

- Do I expect great things of myself?
- Do I expect to do the little things very well?
- Do I expect those little things done well to pave the way to big things done with excellence?

Expect great things of yourself!

344

IF YOU ARE THINKING STRAIGHT, NO ONE CAN FOOL YOU WITH A CURVE.

This is a vitamin we all need to take on a daily basis. Keep your thinking straight – keep moving forward. Do the right things in the right way, every day.

I DON'T FEEL LIKE I NEED A VACATION
TO GET AWAY FROM IT ALL. I JUST LIKE
WHAT I'M DOING.

[Tony Bennett]

If you like what you are doing, you will never have to work
another day in your life.

346

CONDITIONS ARE NEVER JUST RIGHT.
PEOPLE WHO DELAY ACTION UNTIL ALL
FACTORS ARE FAVORABLE ARE THE KIND
WHO DO NOTHING.

[William Feather - Author and Publisher]

Doing nothing for fear of making a mistake is the biggest
mistake of all. Feelings always follow actions. Get into action
and you'll feel better. Things will change in your favor.

Set your goals, then, start reaching your goals.

COURAGE CREATES SOLUTIONS. LEAP, AND THE NET WILL APPEAR.

[Robin Crow - Musician and Entrepreneur]

Keep developing your courage on a daily basis. Take the first step and there'll be someone there to help you take the second step.

Tentative actions will always get you tentative results. On the other hand, strong, dynamic actions will always be rewarded.

348

DON'T MEASURE YOURSELF BY WHAT
YOU'VE ACCOMPLISHED, BUT BY WHAT
YOU SHOULD HAVE ACCOMPLISHED WITH
YOUR ABILITY.

[Coach John Wooden]

Coach Wooden won more national titles than any college
coach in history. At one stretch, he won seven in a row.

He was always more interested in the young athletes playing
to the best of their ability than he was the final score. He
wanted his players to be at their best and play up to their
ability.

WORK HARD, IT WILL CURE ALMOST ALL YOUR PROBLEMS.

[Jack Kinder, Sr. - Excerpt from 50 Lessons In 50 Years - Garry Kinder]

My dad taught me and my brother, Jack, to work hard. He would say to us, "Be known around town as a person who's a hard worker. People like to do business with hard workers. They like to do business with people who are serious about their business."

He also taught us how to make money – and there is a difference between working hard and making money.

Let's bring back the days when honesty, hard work, commitment and loyalty reigned supreme.

350

UNTIL A PERSON CAN SAY DEEPLY AND
HONESTLY, "I AM WHAT I AM TODAY
BECAUSE OF THE CHOICES I MADE
YESTERDAY," THAT PERSON CANNOT SAY,
"I CHOOSE OTHERWISE."

[Steven Covey]

Dr. William T. Beadles said, "Make all major decisions based
on how they will affect you 15 years from today. Do this and
you'll make very few mistakes."

Why?

Because stopping to consider the long-term consequences of
any action is basic to choosing wisely. If you have a major
decision to make, it becomes even more important that you
weigh the outcome with your long-terms goals and dreams in
mind. This also helps you determine just how important the
decision really is. Does it matter in the long run?

Once you make a decision, make it right. Stick to it!

IT'S NOT THE WILL TO WIN, BUT THE WILL TO PREPARE TO WIN THAT MAKES THE DIFFERENCE.

[Bear Bryant]

A Chicago Tribune editor posed this question to Sen. Everett M. Dirksen, the Republican Whip in the senate for many years, "You've been the confidant of four presidents, you've known the great and near great in this world. Who would you say is the greatest person alive today?"

Without hesitation, the Senator said, "It's somebody you never heard about before. It's a mother who gets up and gets her children prepared for school. It's a farmer down in southern Illinois who goes out and plows the ground with nobody cheering, nobody supervising."

This is the way it is with planning and preparation – no one cheering, no one applauding. You have to do it behind closed doors.

352

IN THE END, IT'S NOT THE YEARS IN
YOUR LIFE THAT COUNT, IT'S THE LIFE IN
YOUR YEARS.

[Abraham Lincoln]

The old cliché is still true, it's not the size of the dog in
the fight, it's the size of the fight in the dog. Every day, fill
yourself with enthusiasm, determination, and the will to get
the job done.

Finish strong! Start strong!

VISION WITHOUT TASK IS A DREAM.
TASK WITHOUT VISION IS DRUDGERY.
GOALS REQUIRE ACTION PLANS TO TURN
INTO RESULTS.

[Dr. O.S. Hawkins]

Goal setting is the initial cause of which success is the final effect.

Set two kinds of goals – committed minimum and superior. Your minimum goals are what you must do for the year. They are what you will do regardless. Your minimum goals are committed goals. They are set realistically high and require a complete commitment to their achievement. There is no room for compromise with your minimum goals.

Your superior goals are flavored with optimism. These are the numbers you want to reach over and above your minimum goals. Superior goals are bonus goals.

NEVER BE A QUITTER. QUITTERS NEVER WIN, AND WINNERS NEVER QUIT!

Pete Strudwick, a 50-year old Californian, had an ambition to be a marathon runner. This determined competitor has run and completed more than 40 marathons, including the Boston Marathon - and he has no feet. No feet! Pete runs on stumps.

When asked, "Pete, how do you run 26 miles with no feet?" he replied, "You don't lean backwards!"

In order for you to realize your full potential, develop the kind of persistence that comes only from a made-up mind. By the force of their convictions, successful people wring success from the most adverse circumstances.

LET EVERYTHING HAVE ITS PLACE; LET EACH PART OF YOUR BUSINESS HAVE ITS TIME.

Think about the most successful people you know for a moment. For the most part, successful people are ruthless with their time. They take the time to do the inglorious task of planning. Getting and staying organized is grueling, but without it, you are on a collision course with failure.

Set aside a specific time each week for self-organization. You may be thinking this isn't for you - you don't have time to devote a morning to planning - you don't want to be tied down to a schedule. Here's good news for you: You are already living on a schedule. And, if it's not a planned one, it's probably a poor one!

I adhere to a weekly plan, as well as a daily "To Do" list, which I follow religiously. I like to think of it as planning to wake up employed! Plan your work and work your plan. Your enthusiasm and confidence will soar when you take the time to get and stay organized!

356

MY GREATEST DISCOVERY: WE BECOME
WHAT WE THINK ABOUT MOST OF THE
TIME.

[Earl Nightingale]

Of the many words in all the languages of the world, what
word would you say is the most important when it comes to
success? According to the experts, it's the word "attitude."
The dictionary defines the word "attitude" as a noun meaning
"position, disposition, or manner with regard to a person or
thing."

Philosophies for keeping your thinking correct:
• It can be done! Make this your motto.
• Use perpetual optimism as a force multiplier.
• Be careful what you choose; you may get it.
• Don't let adverse facts stand in the way of a good decision.
• Check out the small things.
• Don't take counsel of your fears. Remain calm.
• Share credit.
• Avoid having your ego so close to your position that when
   your position falls, your ego goes with it.
• Sometimes being responsible means people will be mad at
   you.
• It ain't as bad as you think. It will look better in the
   morning.

ALL EMPOWERMENT EXISTS IN THE PRESENT MOMENT.

Consider moments when you were at your best, and you will find that you were right there in the moment, fully and completely present. If you dwell only on "what was" or "what will be," you will miss the power of "what is."

Spencer Johnson, co-author of The One Minute Manager, talks about this important truth in his brilliant parable, "The Precious Present." In the story, an older man's wisdom launches a young boy on a lifelong search for the "Precious Present." Finally, he discovers what the old man was trying to tell him: To learn from the past is good, but to live there is a waste. To plan for the future is good, but to live there is a waste. You are happiest and most productive in life when you are living in the present.

All highly effective people have learned to respect the power of the present. They have discovered that analyzing the past and planning the future is not enough; they must also nurture the present and celebrate its victories.

Excerpt from The Heart of a Leader, Ken Blanchard

358

THOUGH NO ONE CAN GO BACK AND MAKE A BRAND NEW START, ANYONE CAN START FROM NOW AND MAKE A BRAND NEW ENDING.

It's how you finish, not how you start.

Make up your mind to finish strong in everything you do.

LIVE LIFE WITH A PURPOSE. LEARN AS A WAY OF LIFE. LEAD TO MAKE A DIFFERENCE.

[Don Soderquist]

Most all research shows that people who have a purpose in life, a high calling, do better than those who don't.

The great ones develop a passion for a purpose and keep learning as a way of life.

Everybody is a leader. It's not what your station is in life. Lead to make a difference.

360

BLESSED ARE THE FLEXIBLE, FOR THEY SHALL NOT BE BENT OUT OF SHAPE.

We don't want to be so set in our ways that we aren't open to new ideas and better ways of doing what we've been doing.

361

HE WHO IS SURETY FOR A STRANGER
SHALL SMART FOR IT: AND HE THAT
HATETH SURETISHIP IS SURE.

[Proverbs 11:15 - KJV]

Shakespeare said, "A lender nor a borrower be." Strive to get
out of debt as early as possible.

When it comes to loaning money and endorsing notes, follow
Proverbs 11:15. Be sure you know a person well before you
vouch for his credit! Better to refuse than to suffer later.

362

WE DO NOT REMEMBER DAYS, BUT MOMENTS.

Life moves fast. Enjoy your precious moments.

Take time to enjoy your family and those precious moments that can never be played back.

PERSEVERANCE AND PERSISTENCE
IN SPITE OF ALL OBSTACLES,
DISCOURAGEMENTS AND
IMPOSSIBILITIES—IT IS THIS THAT IN ALL
DISTINGUISHES THE STRONG SOUL FROM
THE WEAK.

[Thomas Carlyle]

Permanence – sticking with the program represents staying
power. This means never giving up. These are words you
want to live by, words that you want your friends to use to
describe you.

364

WE HAVE A GREATER NEED TO BE
REMINDED THAN WE DO TO BE
INFORMED.

[Peter Drucker]

Peter Drucker was a great man. He taught the basic
fundamentals of management right up until his time to die.
He loved this philosophy and talked about it often. Once
people know the fundamentals, they just have to be reminded
to use them over and over again.

HARD WORK SPOTLIGHTS THE CHARACTER OF PEOPLE; SOME TURN UP THEIR SLEEVES, SOME TURN UP THEIR NOSES, AND SOME DON'T TURN UP AT ALL.

The great triumphs of your life will be the rewards of your persistence. Never depend on your genius to carry you. If you have talent, improve it. If you have none, develop it. But, do not depend on it.

Filmmaker Bud Greenspan tells the story of packing up his cameras after the men's marathon at the Mexico City Olympics. Suddenly, a reporter ran up to him, "You ought to film this one." Greenspan looked up and into the darkened stadium hobbled a participant, his right leg bandaged in two places. The man winced with every step. The race had been over for more than an hour, but John Stephen Akhwari of Tanzania still ran. The few hundred spectators who had lingered in the stadium began to clap, slowly and steadily, as Akhwari struggled to the finish line. When finally he stumbled across the finish line, clutching his damaged leg with both hands, the small crowd roared.

Greenspan had recorded every painful, triumphant moment of that emotional, courageous finish. "I asked him, 'Why'd you do this? You were in such pain, and you couldn't win,'" Greenspan recalled. "He looked at me like I was crazy. **'Mr. Greenspan, I don't think you understand. My country did not send me 5,000 miles to start the race. They sent me 5,000 miles to finish it!'"**

LIFE IS NOT SO MUCH A FIGHT TO BE FOUGHT, A GAME TO BE PLAYED OR A PRIZE TO BE WON. IT'S MORE NEARLY A WORK TO BE DONE AND A LEGACY TO BE LEFT.

[William Arthur Ward]

Leaders in all walks of life are forward looking. They have a clear sense of where they are and where they are committed to go. They follow conscientiously and continuously their plan for shaping their futures!

I judge the major decisions for shaping your future to be the following:

1. **What is your passion - long range?** Have you written out your Personal Mission Statement?
2. **Are you excited about what you're doing?** How are you feeling about your progress and future?
3. **Are you satisfied with what you're becoming?** Are you living the balanced life?
4. **How do you plan to achieve financial security?** How much money will you need?
5. **Are you contributing to the well-being of a larger community?** How will you achieve significance, as well as success?
6. **Where will you get your motivation?** What mentors and models will you have?
7. **When your epitaph is written, how will you want it to read?** How do you want to be remembered?

Begin to shape your future today!